Going to Egg Island

Adventures in Grouping and Place Values

Part of the Series

Math in a Cultural Context:

Lessons Learned from Yup'ik Eskimo Elders

Grade 2

Also appropriate for Grade 1

Jerry Lipka

Developed by University of Alaska Fairbanks, Fairbanks, Alaska

 **Detselig Enterprises Ltd**
Calgary, Alberta, Canada

Going to Egg Island: Adventures in Grouping and Place Values
© 2003 University of Alaska Fairbanks

National Library of Canada Cataloguing in Publication Data

Lipka, Jerry.

Going to Egg Island [kit] : adventures in grouping and place values: a math curriculum for first and second grade.—(Math in a cultural context : lessons learned from Yup'ik Eskimo elders)

Includes bibliographical references.

ISBN 1-55059-245-9

1. Mathematics—Study and teaching (Primary) 2. Yupik Eskimos—Study and teaching (Primary) I. Title. II. Series.

QA135.6.L56 2003   372.7'044   C2002-911537-X

Math in a Cultural Context: Lessons Learned from Yup'ik Eskimo Elders© was developed at the University of Alaska Fairbanks. This work was supported in part by the National Science Foundation Grant No. 9618099 and the project's title was Adapting Yup'ik Elders' Knowledge: Pre-K-to-6th Math and Instructional Materials Development.

This project was sponsored, in part, by the National Science Foundation
Opinions expressed are those of the authors and not necessarily those of the Foundation

This project was also sponsored, in part, by the University of Alaska Fairbanks
Alaska Schools Research Fund and the Bristol Bay Curriculum Project

Detselig Enterprises Ltd. acknowledges the financial support of the Government of Canada through the Book Publishing Industry Development Program (BPIDP) for our publishing activities. We also acknowledge the support of the Alberta Foundation for the Arts for our publishing program.

Detselig Enterprises Ltd.
210-1220 Kensington Rd. N.W., Calgary, AB, T2N 3P5
Phone: (403) 283-0900/Fax: (403) 283-6947/E-mail: temeron@telusplanet.net
www.temerondetselig.com

ISBN: 1-55059-245-9
SAN: 115-0324
Printed in Canada.

MATH IN A CULTURAL CONTEXT©

MCC

Principal Investigator and Series Editor:
Jerry Lipka
Project Mathematicians:
Barbara Adams and Susan Addington
Project Manager: Flor Banks
Project Illustrator: Putt (Elizabeth) Clark
Project Layout: Sarah McGowan, Beverly
Peterson, Sue Mitchell
Project Yup'ik Educational Consultants:
Ferdinand Sharp and Evelyn Yanez

Curriculum Writers
Barbara Adams
Deborah Moses
Jane Weber

Evaluation and Assessment
Jo Ann Izu
Kay Gilliland

Folklorist
Ben Orr

***Graduate Research Assistants
and Classroom Observers***
Randi Berlinger
Sandra Wildfeuer

Math Consultants
Clark Bartley
Betsy Brenner
Kay Gilliland
Richard Lehrer
Peter Wiles
Claudia Zaslavsky

Teachers Piloting the Module
Rebecca Adams
Shannon Clouse
Pete Isaacson
Elizabeth Lake
Sheryl Martin
Rich Merritt
Judy Morotti
Sandi Pendergrast
Sassa Peterson
John Purcell
Sharlee Reabold
Nancy Sharp
Sheryl Stevens

Editing
Marie Beaver
Sue Mitchell
Katherine Mulcrone

Technical Support
Dennis Schall

Yup'ik Elder Consultants
Mary Active
Henry Alakayak
Annie Blue
Frederick George
George Moses

Yup'ik Translators
Eliza Orr
Ferdinand Sharp
Nastasia Wahlberg
Evelyn Yanez

Table of Contents

Acknowledgements

The supplemental math series *Math in a Cultural Context: Lessons Learned from Yup'ik Eskimo Elders* is based on traditional and present day wisdom and is dedicated to the late Mary George of Akiachak, Alaska. Mary contributed to every aspect of this long-term project, from her warm acceptance of people from all walks of life to her unique ideas and ways of putting together traditional Yup'ik knowledge with modern Western knowledge. Mary's contributions permeate this work. Without the dedication and perseverance of Mary and her husband Frederick George, who tirelessly continues to work with this project, this work would not be possible.

In addition, for the past twenty-two years I have had the pleasure to work with and learn from Evelyn Yanez of Togiak, Alaska; Nancy and Ferdinand Sharp and Anecia and Jonah Lomack of Manokotak, Alaska; Linda Brown of Ekwok and Fairbanks, Alaska; Sassa Peterson of Homer, Alaska; and Margie Hastings of New Stuyahok, Alaska. Their contributions are immeasurable, as is their friendship. My long-term relationship with elders who embraced this work wholeheartedly has made this difficult endeavor pleasurable as we learn from each other. In particular, I would like to acknowledge Henry Alakayak of Manokotak, Alaska, who has been there for this project and has given unselfishly so that others could prosper from his knowledge; equally unselfishly contributing are Lilly and John Pauk of Manokotak, and Annie Blue, Mary Bavilla, Mary Active, and Emma Nanalook from Togiak—they came with stories that enriched us. Also Sam Ivan of Akiak, Joshua Phillip and George Moses of Akiachak, and Anuska Nanalook and Anecia and Mike Toyukak of Manokotak all provided knowledge about many aspects of traditional life, from Anecia's gifted storytelling and storyknifing to kayaks and other traditional Yup'ik crafts to countless stories on how to survive.

Our dedicated staff, especially Flor Banks, whose highly refined organizational skills, determination to get the job done, and motivation to move this project forward from reading and editing manuscripts to holding the various pieces of this project together, has been an irreplaceable asset, and she has done it all with a smile. To Putt Clark, graphic artist extraordinaire, who kept up with every demand and produced more and better artwork than anyone could have hoped for and has worked with this project from the beginning to end—thank you. To Barbara Adams for her clear-headed thinking and her mathematical insights that contributed so much depth to these modules. To Val Barber who joined us to write a module and ended up taking on more and more work—thanks Val for a job well done. To Sandra Wildfeuer, a doctoral student in education, who has found a place where she uses her talents in mathematics to create modules in this series. I would like to thank Eliza and Ben Orr for producing the Yup'ik Glossary that accompanies this project and for all their hard work, and to Nastasia Wahlberg for translating so many meetings over the years. I wish to thank Lorrine (Nanalook) Masterman who provided us with the original "Egg Island" story and to Cindy Hardy for the excellent job she did in completing this project.

I wish to acknowledge Kay Gilliland for her unflagging, hardworking dedication to this project. A special thanks to Sandi Pendergrast, Sheryl Martin, and John Purcell for allowing us into their classrooms and for the wonderful ideas that they contributed to this project. To the Fairbanks North Star Borough School District, the Lower Yukon School District, the Yupiit School District, the St. Marys School District, the

Anchorage School District, the Yukon Flats School District, and to the Southwest Region Schools for their cooperation in piloting modules. To all the other math writers, project and pilot teachers, and elders who have assisted this project.

To Roger Norris-Tull, dean of the School of Education, University of Alaska Fairbanks, who supported this work generously. Sharon Nelson Barber, West Ed, who has supported this work in spirit and in action for more than a decade. I wish to thank Sue Mitchell for her final editing and page layout work.

Last but not least to my loving wife, Janet Schichnes, who supported me in countless ways that allowed me to complete this work and to my loving children, Alan and Leah, who shared me with so many other people, but I appreciated all the more the wonderful time we did spend together.

Although this has been a long-term collaborative endeavor, I hope that we have taken a small step to meet the desires of the elders for the next generation to be flexible thinkers able to effectively function in the Yup'ik and Western worlds.

Introduction

Math in a Cultural Context

Lessons Learned from Yup'ik Eskimo Elders

Introduction to the Series

Math in a Cultural Context: Lessons Learned from Yup'ik Eskimo Elders1 is a supplemental math curriculum based on the traditional wisdom and practices of the Yup'ik Eskimo people of southwest Alaska. The kindergarten to sixth-grade math modules that you are about to teach are the result of a decade-long collaboration between math educators, teachers, and Yup'ik Eskimo elders and teachers to connect cultural knowledge to school mathematics. To understand the rich environment from which this curriculum came, imagine traveling on a snowmachine over the frozen tundra and finding your way based on the position of the stars in the night sky. Or, in summer, paddling a sleek kayak across open waters shrouded in fog, yet knowing which way to travel toward land by the wave's pattern. Or imagine building a kayak or making clothing and accurately sizing them by visualizing or using body measures. This is a small sample of the activities that modern Yup'ik people engage in. The embedded mathematics formed the basis for this series of supplemental math modules. Each module is independent and lasts from three to eight weeks.

From 1999 through the spring of 2002, students who used these modules consistently outperformed students who used their regular math textbooks, at statistically significant levels. This was true for both urban and rural students, both Caucasian and Alaska Native students. We believe that this supplemental curriculum will motivate your students and strengthen their mathematical understanding because of the engaging content, hands-on approach to problem-solving, and the emphasis on mathematical communication. Further, these modules build on students' everyday experience and intuitive understandings, particularly in geometry, which is underrepresented in school.

The modules explore the everyday application of mathematics skills such as grouping, approximating, measuring, proportional thinking, informal geometry, and counting in base twenty and then present these in terms of formal mathematics. Students move from the concrete and applied to more formal and abstract math. The activities are designed to meet the following goals:

- Students learn to solve mathematical problems that support an in-depth understanding of mathematical concepts.
- Students derive mathematical formulas and rules from concrete and practical applications.
- Students become flexible thinkers because they learn that there is more than one method of solving a mathematical problem.
- Students learn to communicate and think mathematically while they demonstrate their understanding to peers.
- Students learn content across the curriculum, since the lessons comprise Yup'ik Eskimo culture, literacy, geography, and science.

Beyond meeting some of the content (mathematics) and process standards of the National Council of Teachers of Mathematics (2000), the curriculum design and its activities respond to the needs of diverse learners. Many activities are designed for group work. One of the strategies for using group work is to provide leadership opportunities to students who may not typically be placed in that role. Also, the modules tap into a wide array of intellectual abilities—practical, creative, and analytic. We assessed modules that were tested in rural Alaska, urban Alaska, and suburban California, and found that students who were only peripherally involved in math became more active participants.

Students learn to reason mathematically by constructing models and analyzing practical tasks for their embedded mathematics. This enables them to generate and discover mathematical rules and formulas. In this way, we offer students a variety of ways to engage the math material through practical activity, spatial visual learning, analytic thinking, and creative thinking. They are constantly encouraged to communicate mathematically by presenting their understandings while other students are encouraged to provide alternate solutions, strategies, and counter arguments. This process also strengthens their deductive reasoning.

To summarize, the curriculum design includes strategies that engage students:
- cognitively, so that students use a variety of thinking strategies (analytic, creative, and practical);
- socially, so that students with different social, cognitive, and mathematical skills use those strengths to lead and help solve mathematical problems;
- pedagogically, so that students explore mathematical concepts and communicate and learn to reason mathematically by demonstrating their understanding of the concepts; and
- practically, as students apply or investigate mathematics to solve problems from their daily lives.

Pedagogical Approach Used in the Modules

The organization of the modules follows five distinctly different approaches to teaching and learning that converge into one system.

Expert-Apprentice Modeling

The first approach, expert-apprentice modeling, comes from Yup'ik elders and teachers and is supported by research in anthropology and education. Many lessons begin with the teacher (the expert) demonstrating a concept to the students (the apprentices). Following the theoretical position of the Russian psychologist Vygotsky (cited in Moll, 1990) and expert Yup'ik teachers (Lipka and Yanez, 1998) and elders, students begin to appropriate the knowledge of the expert (teacher), as the teacher and the more adept apprentices help other students learn. This establishes a collaborative classroom setting in which student-to-student and student-to-teacher dialogues are part of the classroom fabric.

Reform-oriented Approach

The second pedagogical approach emphasizes student collaboration in solving "deeper" problems (Ma, 1999). This approach is supported by research in math classrooms and particularly by recent international studies (Stevenson et al., 1990; Stigler and Hiebert, 1998) that strongly suggest that math problems should be more in-depth and challenging and that students should understand the underlying principles, not merely use procedures competently. The modules present complex problems (two-step open-ended problems) that require students to think more deeply about mathematics.

Multiple Intelligences

Further, the modules tap into students' multiple intelligences. While some students may learn best from hands-on, real-world related problems, others may learn best when abstracting and deducing. This module provides opportunities to guide both modalities. Robert Sternberg's work (1997; 1998) influenced the development of these modules. He has consistently found that students who are taught so that they use their analytic, creative, and practical intelligences will outperform students who are taught using one modality, most often analytic. Thus, we have shaped our activities to engage students in this manner.

Mathematical Argumentation and Deriving Rules

The modules support a math classroom environment in which students explore the underlying mathematical rules as they solve problems. Through structured classroom communication, students will learn to work collaboratively in a problem-solving environment in which they learn to both appreciate alternative solutions strategies and evaluate these strategies and solutions. They present their mathematical solutions to their peers. Through discrepancies in strategies and solutions, students will communicate with and help each other to understand their reasoning and mathematical decisions. Mathematical discussions are encouraged to strengthen their mathematical and logical thinking as students share their findings. This requires classroom norms that support student communication, learning from errors, and viewing errors as an opportunity to learn rather than to criticize. The materials in the modules (see Materials section) constrain the possibilities, guide students in a particular direction, and increase their chances of understanding the mathematical concepts. Students are given the opportunity to support their conceptual understanding by practicing it in the context of a particular problem.

Familiar and Unfamiliar Contexts Challenge Students' Thinking

By working in unfamiliar settings and facing new and challenging problems, students learn to think creatively. They gain confidence in their ability to solve both everyday problems and abstract mathematical questions, and their entire realm of knowledge and experience expands. Further, by making the familiar unfamiliar and by working on novel problems, students are encouraged to connect what they learn from one setting (everyday problems) with mathematics in another setting. For example, most sixth-grade students know about rectangles and how to calculate the area of a rectangle, but if you ask students to go outside and find the four corners of an eight-foot-by twelve-foot-rectangle without using rulers or similar instruments, they are faced with a challenging problem. As they work through this everyday application (which is needed to build any rectangular structure) and as they "prove" to their classmates that they do, in fact, have a rectangular base, they expand their knowledge of rectangles. In effect they must shift their thinking from considering rectangles as physical entities or as prototypical examples to understanding the salient properties of a rectangle. Similarly, everyday language, conceptions, and intuition may, in fact, be in the way of mathematical understanding and the precise meaning of mathematical terms. By treating familiar knowledge in unfamiliar ways, students explore and confront their own mathematical understandings and they begin to understand the world of mathematics.

These major principles guide the overall pedagogical approach to the modules.

The Organization of the Modules

The curriculum comprises twelve modules for kindergarten through sixth grade. Modules are divided into sections: activities, explorations, and exercises, with some variation between each module. Supplementary information is included in Cultural Notes, Teacher Notes, and Math Notes. Each module follows a particular cultural story line, and the mathematics connects directly to it. Some modules are designed around a children's story, and an illustrated text is included for the teacher to read to the class.

The module is a teacher's manual. It begins with a general overview of the activities ahead, an explanation of the math and pedagogy of the module, teaching suggestions, and a historical and cultural overview of the curriculum in general and of the specific module. Each activity includes a brief introductory statement, an estimated duration, goals, materials, any preclass preparatory instructions for the teacher, and the procedures for the class to carry out the activity. Assessments are placed at various stages, both intermittently and at the end of activities.

Illustrations help to enliven the text. Yup'ik stories and games are interspersed and enrich the mathematics. Overhead masters, worksheet masters, assessments, and suggestions for additional materials are attached at the end of each activity. An overhead projector is necessary. Blackline masters that can be made into overhead transparencies are an important visual enhancement of the activities, stories, and games. Supplemental aids—colored posters, coloring books, and CD ROMs—are attached separately or may be purchased elsewhere. Such visual aids also help to further classroom discussion and understanding. CD-ROMs can be found at http://www.uaf.edu/educ/Grants/html/hp.html.

Resources and Materials Required to Teach the Modules

Materials

The materials and tools limit the range of mathematical possibilities, guiding students' explorations so that they focus upon the intended purpose of the lesson. For example, in the *Elastic Geometry* module, latex sheets are used to explore concepts of topology. Students can manipulate the latex to the degree necessary to discover the mathematics of the various activities and apply the rules of topology.

For materials and learning tools that are more difficult to find or that are directly related to unique aspects of this curriculum, we provide detailed instructions for the teacher and students on how to make those tools. For example, in *Going to Egg Island: Adventures in Grouping and Place Values,* students use a base-twenty abacus. Although the project has produced and makes available a few varieties of wooden abaci, detailed instructions are provided for the teacher and students on how to make a simple, inexpensive, and usable abacus with beads and pipe cleaners.

Each module and each activity lists all of the materials and learning tools necessary to carry it out. Some of the tools are expressly mathematical, such as interlocking centimeter cubes, abaci, and compasses. Others are particular to the given context of the problem, such as latex and black and white geometric pattern pieces. Many of the materials are items a teacher will probably have on hand, such as paper, markers, scissors, and rulers. Students learn to apply and manipulate the materials. The value of caring for the materials is underscored by the precepts of subsistence, which is based on processing raw materials and foods with maximum use and minimum waste. Periodically, we use food as part of an activity. In these instances, we encourage minimal waste.

Videos

To more vividly convey the knowledge of the elders that underlies the entire curriculum, we have produced a few videos to accompany some of the modules. For example, the *Going to Egg Island: Adventures in Grouping and Place Values* module includes videos of Yup'ik elders demonstrating some traditional Yup'ik games. We also have footage and recordings of the ancient chants that accompanied these games. The videos are available on CD-ROM and are readily accessible for classroom use.

Yup'ik Language Glossary and Math Terms Glossary

To help teachers and students get a better feel for the Yup'ik language, its sounds, and the Yup'ik words used to describe mathematical concepts in this curriculum, we have developed a Yup'ik glossary on CD-ROM. Each word is recorded in digital form and can be played back in Yup'ik. The context of the word is provided, giving teachers and students a better sense of the Yup'ik concept, not just its Western "equivalent." Pictures and illustrations often accompany the word for additional clarification.

Values

There are many important Yup'ik values associated with each module. The elders counsel against waste; they value listening, learning, working hard, being cooperative, and passing knowledge on to others. These values are expressed in the contents of the Yup'ik stories that accompany the modules, in the cultural notes, and in various activities. Similarly, Yup'ik people as well as other traditional people continue to produce, build, and make crafts from raw materials. Students who engage in these modules also learn how to make simple mathematical tools fashioned around such themes as Yup'ik border patterns and building model kayaks, fish racks, and smokehouses. Students learn to appreciate and value other cultures.

Cultural Notes

Most of the mathematics used in the curriculum comes from our direct association and long-term collaboration with Yup'ik Eskimo elders and teachers. We have included many cultural notes to more fully describe and explain the purposes, origins, and variations associated with a particular traditional activity. Each module is based on a cultural activity and follows a Yup'ik cultural storyline, along which the activities and lessons unfold. The activities reflect the various aspects or stages of the particular activity.

Math Notes

We want to ensure that teachers who may want to teach these materials but feel unsure of some of the mathematical concepts will feel supported by the math notes. These provide background material to help teachers better understand the mathematical concepts presented in the activities and exercises of each module. For example, in the *Perimeter and Area* module, the math notes give a detailed description of a rectangle and describe the geometric proofs one would apply to ascertain whether or not a shape is a rectangle. The *Rectangular Prism* module explores the geometry of three-dimensional objects, and the math notes include information on the geometry of rectangular prisms, including proofs, to facilitate the instructional process. In every module, connections are made between the "formal math," its practical application, and the classroom strategies for teaching the math.

Teacher Notes

The main function of the teacher notes is to bring to awareness the key pedagogical aspects of the lesson. For example, they provide suggestions on how to facilitate students' mathematical understanding through classroom organization strategies, classroom communication, and ways of structuring lessons. Teacher Notes also make suggestions for ways of connecting out-of-school knowledge with schooling.

Assessment

Assessment and instruction are interrelated throughout the modules. Assessments are embedded within instructional activities, and teachers are encouraged to carefully observe, listen, and challenge their students' thinking. We call this active assessment, which allows teachers to assess how well students have learned to solve the mathematical and cultural problems introduced in a module.

Careful attention has been given to developing assessment techniques and tools that evaluate both the conceptual and procedural knowledge of students. We agree with Ma (1999) that having one type of knowledge without the other, or a lack of understanding of the link between the two, will produce only partial understanding. The goal here is to produce relational understanding in mathematics. Instruction and assessment have been developed and aligned to ensure that both types of knowledge are acquired, and this has been accomplished using both traditional and alternative techniques.

The specific details and techniques for assessment when applicable are included within activities. The three main tools for collecting and using assessment data follow.

Journals

Each student can keep a journal for daily entries, consisting primarily of responses to specific activities. Student journals serve as a current record of their work and a long-term record of their increasing mathematical knowledge and ability to communicate this knowledge. Many of the modules and their activities require students to predict, sketch, define, explain, calculate, design, and solve problems. Often, students will be asked to revisit their responses after a series of activities, so that they can appreciate and review what they have learned. Student journals also provide the teacher with insight into their thinking, making it an active tool in the assessment and instructional process.

Observation

Observing and listening to their students lets teachers learn about the strategies that they use to analyze and solve various problems. Listening to informal conversations between students as they work cooperatively on problems provides further insight into their strategies. Through observation, teachers also learn about their students' attitudes toward mathematics and their skills in cooperating with others. Observation is an excellent way to link assessment with instruction.

Adaptive Instruction

The goal of the summary assessment in this curriculum is to adapt instruction to the skills and knowledge needed by a group of students. From reviewing journal notes to simply observing, teachers learn which mathematical processes their students are able to effectively use and which ones they need to practice more. Adaptive assessment and instruction complete the link between assessment and instruction.

An Introduction to the Land and Its People, Geography, and Climate

Flying over the largely uninhabited expanse of southwest Alaska on a dark winter morning, one looks down at a white landscape interspersed with trees, winding rivers, rolling hills, and mountains. One sees a handful of lights sprinkled here, a handful there. Half of Alaska's 600,000-plus population lives in Anchorage. The other half is dispersed among smaller cities such as Fairbanks and Juneau and among the over two hundred rural villages that are scattered across the state. Landing on the village airstrip, which is usually gravel and, in the winter, covered with smooth, hard-packed snow, one is taken to the village by either car or snowmachine. Hardly any villages or regional centers are connected to or by a road system. The major means of transportation between these communities is by small plane, boat, and snow machine, depending on the season.

It is common for the school to be centrally located. Village roads are usually unpaved, and people drive cars, four wheelers, and snow machines. Houses are typically made from modern materials and have electricity and running water. Over the past twenty years, Alaska villages have undergone major changes, both technologically and culturally. Most now have television, a full phone system, modern water and sewage treatment facilities, an airport, and a small store. Some also have a restaurant, and a few even have a small hotel and taxicab service. Access to medical care and public safety are still sporadic, with the former usually provided by a local health care worker and a community health clinic, or by health care workers from larger cities or regional centers who visit on a regular basis. Serious medical emergencies require air evacuation to either Anchorage or Fairbanks.

The Schools

Years of work have gone into making education as accessible as possible to rural communities. Almost every village has an elementary school, and most have a high school. Some also have a higher education satellite facility, computer access to higher education courses, or options that enable students to work on and earn college credits while in their respective home communities. Vocational education is taught in some of the high schools, and there are also special vocational education facilities in some villages. While English has become the dominant language throughout Alaska, many Yup'ik children in the villages of this region still learn Yup'ik at home.

Yup'ik Village Life Today

Most villagers continue to participate in the seasonal rounds of hunting, fishing, and gathering. Although many modern conveniences are located within the village, when one steps outside of its narrow bounds, one is immediately aware of one's vulnerability in this immense and unforgiving land, where one misstep can lead to disaster. Depending upon their location (coastal community, riverine, or interior), villagers hunt and gather the surrounding resources. These include sea mammals, fish, caribou, and many types of berries. The seasonal subsistence calendar illustrates which activities take place during the year (see Fig. 1). Knowledgeable elders know how to cross rivers and find their way through ice fields, navigating the seemingly featureless tundra by using directional indicators such as frozen grass and the constellations in the night sky. All of this can mean the difference between life and death. In the summer, when this largely treeless, moss-and-grass-covered plain thaws into a large swamp dotted with small lakes, the consequences of ignorance, carelessness, and inexperience can be just as devastating. Underwater hazards in the river, such as submerged logs, can capsize a boat, dumping the occupants into the cold, swift current. Overland travel is much more difficult during the warm months due to the marshy ground and many waterways, and one can easily become disoriented and get lost. The sea is also integral to life in this region and requires its own set of skills and specialized knowledge to be safely navigated.

The Importance of the Land: Hunting and Gathering

Basic subsistence skills include knowing how to read the sky to determine the weather and make appropriate travel plans, being able to read the land to find one's way, knowing how to build an emergency shelter and, in the greater scheme, how to hunt and gather food and properly process and store it. In addition, the byproducts of subsistence activities, such as carved walrus tusks, pelts and skins made into clothing or decorative items, and a variety of other utilitarian and arts and crafts products provide an important source of cash for many rural residents.

Hunting and gathering are still of great importance in modern Yup'ik society. A young man's first seal hunt is celebrated; family members who normally live and work in one of the larger cities will often fly home to help when the salmon are running; whole families still gather to go berry picking. The importance of hunting and gathering in daily life is further reflected in the legislative priorities expressed by rural residents in Alaska. These focus on such things as subsistence hunting regulations, fishing quotas, and resource development and environmental issues that affect the well-being of game animals and subsistence vegetation.

Conclusion

We developed this curriculum in a Yup'ik context. The traditional subsistence and other skills of the Yup'ik people incorporate spatial, geometrical, and proportional reasoning and other mathematical reasoning. We have attempted to offer you and your students a new way to approach and apply mathematics while also learning about Yup'ik culture. Our goal has been to present math as practical information that is inherent in everything we do. We hope your students will adopt and incorporate some of this knowledge and add it to the learning base.

We hope you and your students will benefit from the mathematics, culture, geography, and literature embedded in *Math in a Cultural Context: Lessons Learned from Yup'ik Eskimo Elders*. The elders who guided this work emphasized that the next generation of children should be flexible thinkers and leaders. In a small way, we hope that this curriculum guides you and your students along this path.

Tua-ii ingrutuq [This is not the end].

References

Lipka, Jerry, and Evelyn Yanez. 1998. "Identifying and Understanding Cultural Differences: Toward Culturally Based Pedagogy." In *Transforming the Culture of Schools,* edited by Lipka, J., Mohatt, G., and the Ciulistet, 111–137. Mahwah, NJ: Lawrence Erlbaum.

Ma, Liping. 1999. *Knowing and Teaching Elementary Mathematics*. Mahwah, NJ: Lawrence Erlbaum.

Moll, Luis. 1990. *Vygotksy and Education: Instructional Implications and Applications of Sociohistorical Psychology*. Cambridge: Cambridge University Press.

National Council of Teachers of Mathematics. 2000. *Principles and Standards for School Mathematics*. Reston, VA: National Council of Teachers of Mathematics.

Sternberg, Robert. 1997. *Successful Intelligence*. New York: Plume.

Sternberg, Robert. 1998. Principles of Teaching for Successful Intelligence. *Educational Psychologist 33,* 65–72.

Stevenson, Harold, Max Lummis, Shin-Yin Lee, and James Stigler. 1990. *Making the Grade in Mathematics*. Arlington, VA: National Council of Teachers of Mathematics.

Stigler, James, and James Hiebert. 1998. Teaching is a Cultural Activity. *American Educator* 22(4):4–11.

Notes

1. This math series is based on *Adapting Yup'ik Elders' Knowledge: Pre-K-to-6 Math and Instructional Materials Development,* a project sponsored by the National Science Foundation (NSF), award #9618099.

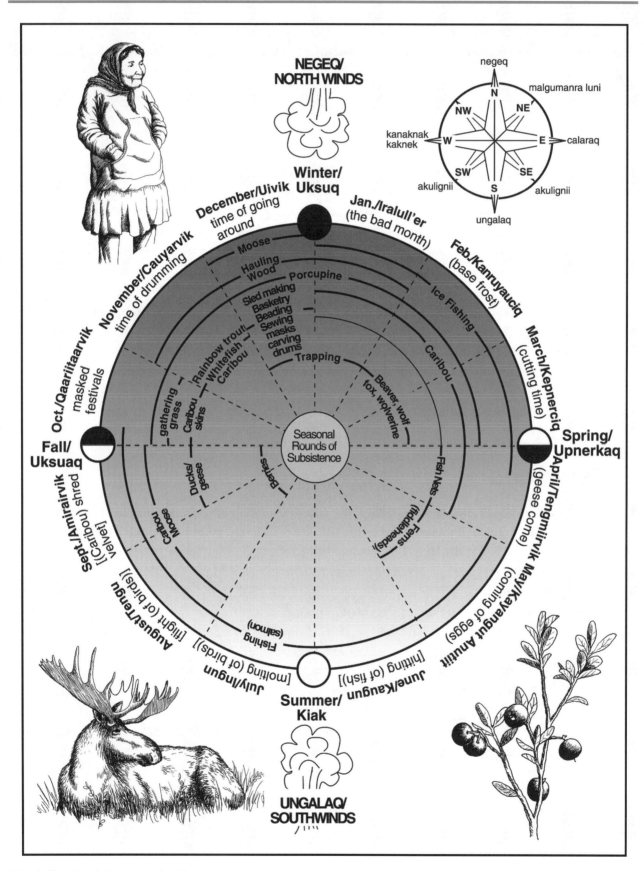

Fig. 1: Yearly subsistence calendar

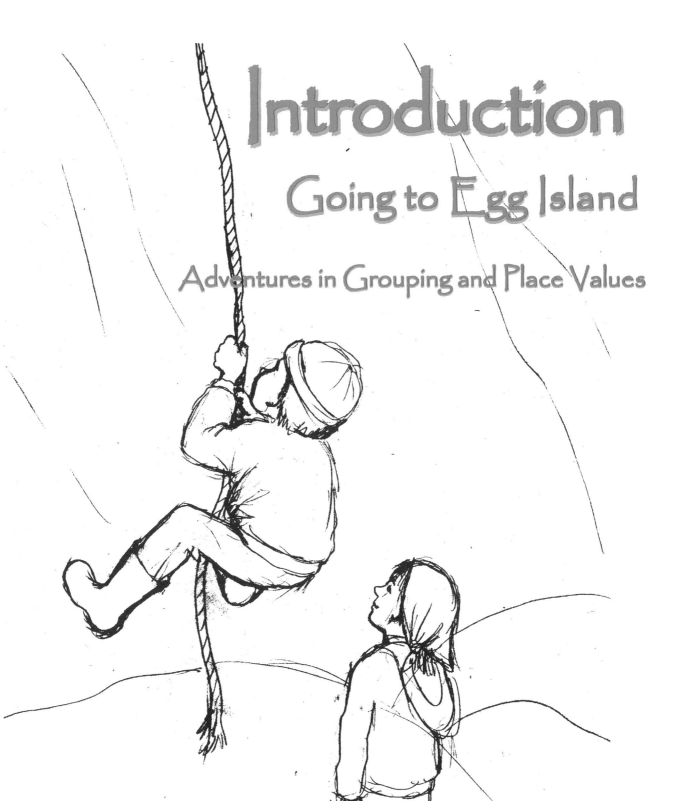

Introduction
Going to Egg Island

Adventures in Grouping and Place Values

Introduction and Overview of the Module

Going to Egg Island: Adventures in Grouping and Place Values is a problem and literacy-based supplemental math module for grades one and two. This module engages students because the background story draws them into the life of a second-grade girl living in a Yup'ik Eskimo community. Based on her intriguing experiences, your students learn as they use novel math tools (such as a Yup'ik abacus) and group objects in a variety of ways; students play traditional Yup'ik games while simultaneously investigating number patterns, and eventually these experiences coalesce into a strong sense of grouping and place values.

Going to Egg Island is an interdisciplinary unit on Yup'ik culture, geography, and biology and is founded on the everyday practices and cultural and traditional knowledge of the Yup'ik Eskimo of southwest Alaska. In a series of problems that are built around a story, with a central theme of villagers gathering sea bird eggs in the spring, your students will learn about and apply the mathematical concepts and skills of counting and grouping two-digit numbers, estimating, measuring, sorting, and place values. Pages four to six show a graphic representation of the module.

Suggested Prior Activities

In this module students count by fives, tens, and twenties. You may want to provide some exposure to "skip counting" through calendar activities, games, songs, or chants that will allow students to grasp the bigger concepts introduced throughout the unit. If your students have not worked with skip counting proceed at a slower pace and build that knowledge while working through this module.

Thoughts on Teaching Grouping and Place Values

Students will gain the most from this unit by making many "aha's" for themselves as they develop their own algorithms and gain a sense of numbers and place values. Critical to students' growing understanding is the teacher facilitating the students' learning, that is, providing enough structure so the student can work semiautonomously, balancing when to provide cues and support and when to allow students to struggle as they discover. The teacher guides them, encouraging students to learn from mistakes and initiating mathematical discussions about what went wrong and what went right. Helping children "construct meaning" can be difficult. There are so many constraints today on teaching to the test as well as having so many different types of learners. Yet research shows that asking open-ended questions like, "Tell me about..." or "Explain your thinking" can give a teacher insight into where the instruction needs to go.

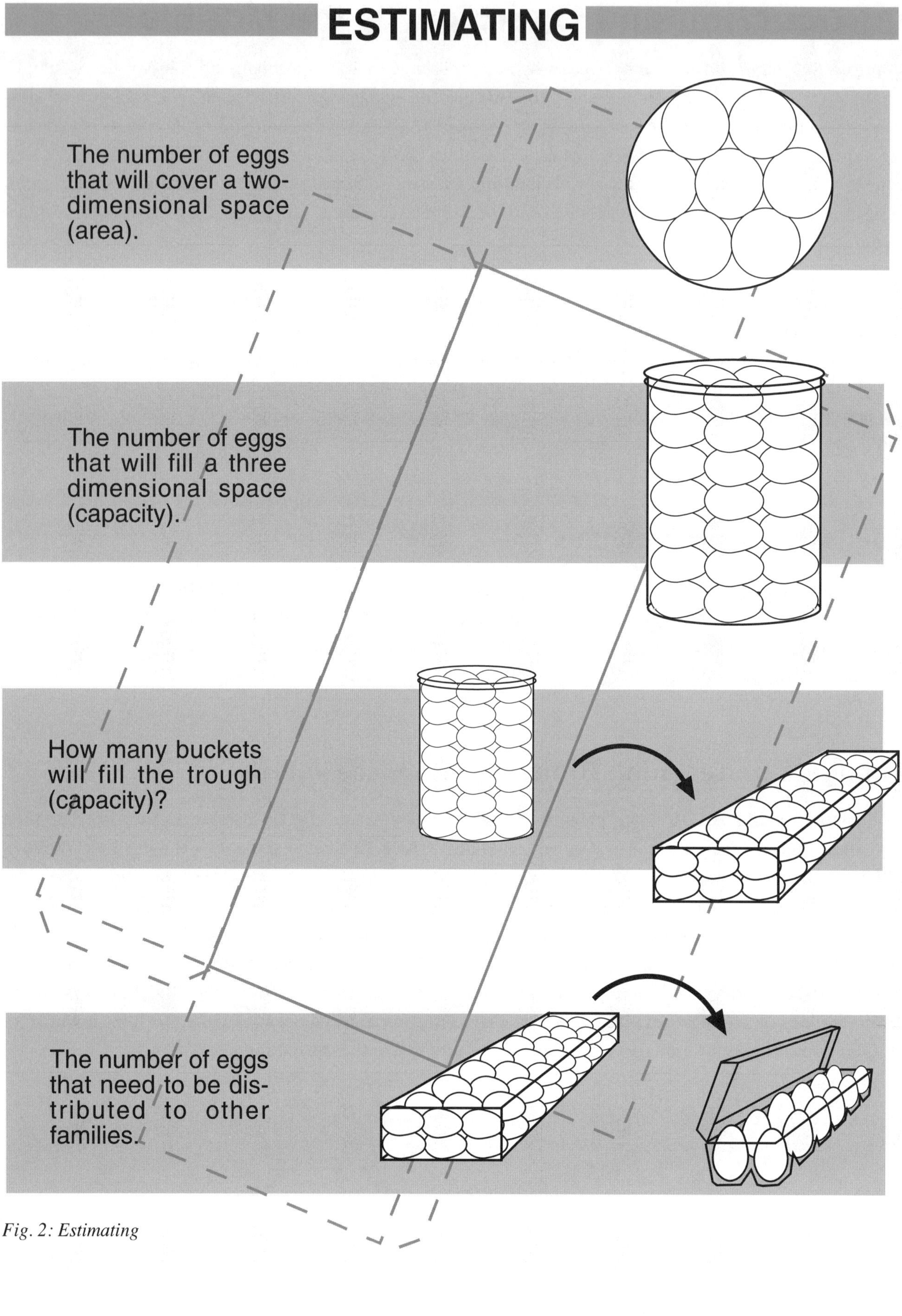

ESTIMATING

The number of eggs that will cover a two-dimensional space (area).

The number of eggs that will fill a three dimensional space (capacity).

How many buckets will fill the trough (capacity)?

The number of eggs that need to be distributed to other families.

Fig. 2: Estimating

GROUPING

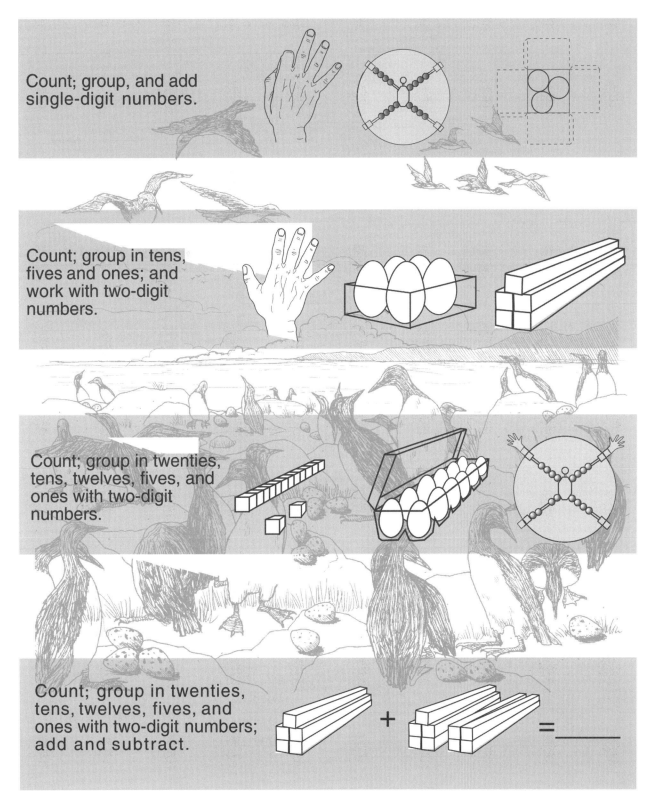

Count; group, and add single-digit numbers.

Count; group in tens, fives and ones; and work with two-digit numbers.

Count; group in twenties, tens, twelves, fives, and ones with two-digit numbers.

Count; group in twenties, tens, twelves, fives, and ones with two-digit numbers; add and subtract.

Fig. 3: Grouping

METHODS OF GROUPING

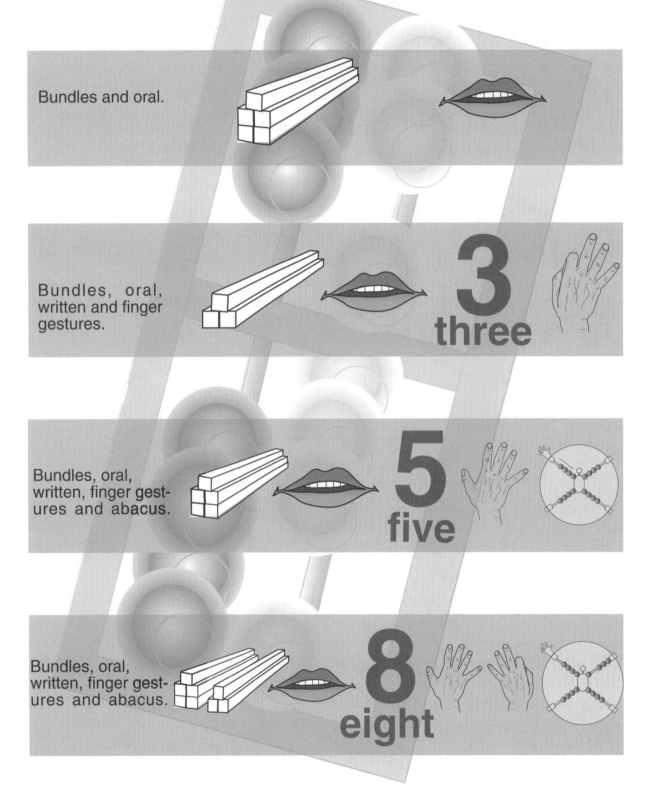

Bundles and oral.

Bundles, oral, written and finger gestures.

Bundles, oral, written, finger gestures and abacus.

Bundles, oral, written, finger gestures and abacus.

Fig. 4: Methods of grouping

Story-Based Approach

The module is presented through the eyes of an eight-year-old girl who is visiting the village from a city. The story *Egg Island* weaves the setting, culture, and math together. It describes the villagers' trip to Egg Island and ties together the nineteen lessons that comprise this module. Six games (two of these are authentic Yup'ik games) give your students further practice with the mathematical concepts presented in this module. These games also increase your students' motivation as they play them in the class and learn more about Yup'ik culture.

Counting the "chicks" they see on Egg Island provides the background for your students to learn to estimate, group, and sort. Through a series of increasingly sophisticated and complex problems, your students will see the connections among the various ways that numbers can be represented. They will move from the concrete to the abstract and learn to become independent of concrete representations of numbers, i.e., eggs, and instead use the abstract symbols, i.e., numerals. Students will learn a number, then represent it ever more abstractly, going from its oral and written representation, to grouping by bundling sticks, to representing the number with finger gestures, to using the number in addition and subtraction problems. Eventually, students will also learn to add and subtract using numerals (symbols).

The story of Egg Island provides additional learning opportunities in social studies, science, history, and geography. Readings from the story begin each lesson and provide your students with lessons that directly involve them with the life, culture, and environment the people in the story are experiencing.

Flexible and Creative Thinking

This module requires your students to engage in flexible and creative thinking and challenges them as they learn both basic math facts and problem-solving skills. The concepts cycle from one lesson to the next, and with each repetition they grow in complexity and sophistication.

Progression of the Math

The math in Problem One, Activity 1, begins with students considering an egg-gathering bucket for their "trip" to Egg Island. The math requires them to estimate the number of eggs that will cover a circle, i.e., a flat, two-dimensional surface, which represents the bottom of the bucket. The students estimate and tally single-digit numbers. In Activity 2, students tackle the more complex problem of estimating capacity, and must estimate how many eggs are needed to fill a container, not just cover its bottom surface. The shape of the container will vary (cylinder or rectangular prism), as will the size of the eggs used to fill it. Because filling the container will require more eggs than covering its bottom surface, students will be counting and grouping double-digit numbers. These early activities are the building blocks for future lessons.

Later in the module, students are introduced to the concept of the abacus. In collaboration with elders who have been associated with this project for more than ten years, we developed and designed an abacus for young children based on the Yup'ik language and how it conveys numbers. The elders were very pleased with this abacus and found that they could use it quite easily. This was developed especially for this project and is based on the traditional Yup'ik system of counting, but the abacus itself was never traditionally used by the Yup'ik. The "Yup'ik" abacus uses the traditional system of counting and grouping, which is based on fives and twenties and relates directly to the human body. Students learn to manipulate specific representations of numeric groupings. The abacus is also introduced because it is a step removed from the body and is a step toward more abstract thinking.

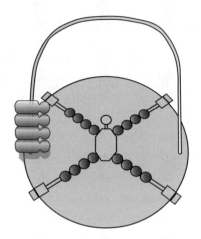

Fig. 5: Yup'ik abacus

Throughout the module, students are challenged to group differently. For example, in American society, groupings of ten are common. However, your students can find other groupings. Eggs are grouped in dozens, i.e. twelves, and Yup'ik people group in fives and twenties. This helps students see that a quantity can be grouped differently, depending upon the "unit" (base) of grouping. For example, grouping the number 40 by 10 would be 4 sets of 10; by 12s it would be 3 sets of 12s with 4 left over; by 20s it would be 2 sets of 20.

Multiple Intelligences

This module taps into your students' multiple intelligences and supports many ways of learning. For example, some students may be adept at paper and pencil problems involving deductive reasoning, others may perform better when called upon to estimate, and others may respond better through the use of tactile objects, such as bundling sticks. Even musical sounds are applied to math. In one practice lesson students must distinguish numerical differences by listening to different drumbeats, each of which represents a different number.

Mathematical Communication

As students work through the lessons, they are encouraged to explain to their peers (both orally and in writing), their methods and processes for arriving at their conclusions. These verbal explanations will help to further their mathematical communication skills and also provide an assessment for the teacher.

This module relies on fairly simple learning materials, which facilitate its presentation and feasibility in a classroom setting.

Research-Based Approach to the Teaching of Numeration

The development of this module is informed by a number of different research perspectives on students' thinking, as they learn to count, add, and subtract numbers. From a Piagetian perspective, the work leans on Kamii (1989) and Piaget (1960) emphasizing students' constructing their own meaning from their experience. These constructions shift and change as students develop more advanced thinking. From the perspective of classroom discourse and students' reflective thinking, Cobb's (1997) and Secada's (1996) research inform this module. Here the role of students' mathematical dialogue is critical to their developing understanding. Research on the mathematical structures (Fuson, 1997; Carpenter, et al., 1998), which are important for students to comprehend the meaning of multidigit addition and subtraction, also guides the development of this module. This work shows that students may at first view numbers as individual units. Later they may conceive of groups of ten instead of individual sets of ones, showing advances in counting by not starting over when they reach ten but by counting on. The teaching approach advocated by Ma (1999) is incorporated to foster a classroom environment in which students learn and explore the fundamental underlying math concepts of grouping and regrouping (composing and decomposing) numbers. Ma envisions a classroom in which the teacher's deeper understanding of math challenges the students' thinking and where students explore, discuss, and challenge one another.

Pedagogy

Constructivist Approach and Classroom Discourse

This module supports a constructivist approach to teaching and learning, where the teacher facilitates the students' thinking and stresses that they find their own solutions to problems. Following the lead of Kamii (1989) and Ma (1999), it is important for students to "invent" their own solutions to single and two-digit arithmetic problems, so that they fully understand how algorithms operate. Students are encouraged to add numbers, such as 19 + 16, as shown below:

```
   19
 + 16
   35
```

They are also encouraged to explore other ways of grouping and adding:

10 + 10 + 10 + [6–1] = 35.

Kamii (p. 77) states that typical invented procedures for students who solve 18 + 13 are listed below:

10+10=20
8+3=11
20 +10=30
30+1=31

10+10=20
8+3=11
28+3=31

Research by Cobb (1997) suggests that the process of having students increasingly reflect and discuss their solutions to two-digit addition and subtraction problems fosters social and self-correcting mechanisms, both for their procedures and answers. The process of reflection, discussion, and discovery helps to empower students in their learning. This module envisions the teacher as a facilitator who promotes students' conceptual understandings by guiding the process of learning.

This research is combined with and informed by long-term work with Yup'ik teachers and elders. It supports a way of teaching that includes teacher demonstrations and modeling and one that facilitates students' independent learning, so that they become autonomous learners. Reflective discourse, or thinking aloud, is an important component for clarifying students' understanding of numbers.

The teaching method brings together an anthropological or cultural perspective and a constructivist approach, as characterized by the work of Vygotsky and adapted to mathematics classrooms by Cobb (1997). The cultural perspective views the importance of cultural tools (the use of everyday artifacts and knowledge) and creating "relevant" ways for students to learn about math tools (base ten materials, rulers, etc.). The strategy of making the familiar unfamiliar for students who are learning base ten, then providing them with a point of comparison as they learn how other cultures group and combine numbers, is applied. This contrastive approach provides those for whom base twenty is familiar with a fresh way of understanding base ten. Students learn by contrast. The familiar (counting and grouping by tens) becomes unfamiliar when countings and groupings are done in twenties.

Classroom Norms and Student Thinking

Second-grade students are already socialized into a culture of school math that values "correct" answers over students' understanding (Ma, 1999). There is no question about the importance of students memorizing math facts, knowing how to use algorithms, and efficiently finding answers to simple math questions. However, without understanding what these "facts" mean, students run the risk of not having a foundation upon which to build their mathematical understanding. Students as young as second graders need to overcome their fears and inhibitions about making mistakes, since mistakes provide them and other students opportunities to learn about their own mathematical thinking and understanding.

In our classroom research, students said that talking about their mathematical thinking isn't math: real math is done on paper and pencil, not through modeling, hands-on activity, or games. This curriculum envisions an approach that values and supports students' thinking through their problem-solving, by observing the processes that students' use while solving problems and having students explain their approaches. Further, when appropriate this module encourages students to invent their own algorithms and procedures. However, we also envision connecting their understanding and procedures to the efficient use of algorithms. As a teacher of this module, one of your roles is to create an environment that encourages and supports students to share their thinking and to learn from each other. This will occur slowly as your students begin to recognize the advantages and importance of understanding mathematics. With practice, the latter becomes familiar. This heightens students' interest, as they realize that numbers and their groupings are socially constructed and follow the specific rules of a given culture.

Why Yup'ik Numeration?

The body is a natural medium for developing young students' understanding of numbers and groupings in general. Traditional Yup'ik counting connects directly to the human body. In the module, counting and grouping are physically and concretely tied to the students' bodies. They will learn that many other cultures also use their bodies to count. This module emphasizes groupings by fives, tens, and twenties. The Yup'ik, and all other Eskimo groups, traditionally count with all their fingers and toes. Students will learn that individual digits represent the "ones," that a hand or a foot represent a "five," and that "a person complete" represents "twenty." Because each "person complete" represents twenty, the Yup'ik system is excellent for teaching students new strategies for grouping, especially those based on concrete connections to the body.

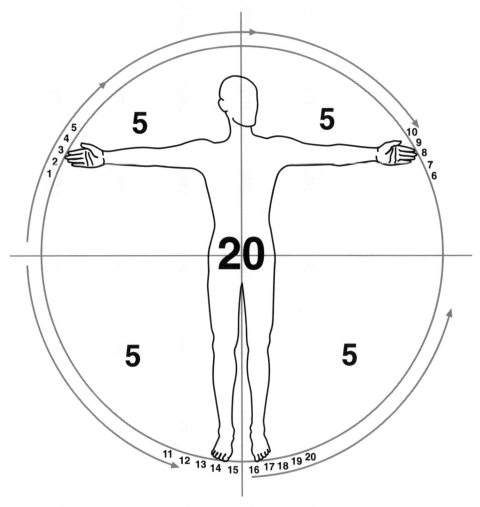

Information gathered from Edward W. Nelson, *The Eskimo About Bering Strait*. 1899, pp. 263–237.

Fig. 6: Yup'ik body counting

Finger Gestures

A traditional Yup'ik way of counting corresponds directly to the human body. Hands, feet, limbs, and the whole body are used to represent cardinalities, and are counted from right to left, beginning with the pinky on the right hand. In the Yup'ik language, as in many other languages, number names are associated with certain finger gestures, which probably developed before, or along with, the words. For example, in the Zulu language of South Africa, counting begins by extending the little finger of the left hand. For "two," the left pinky and ring finger are extended. This succession continues, until the counter reaches "five." The word for "six" means "thumb," and the thumb of the right hand is extended. Again, the succession continues, until the counter reaches "ten" and all ten fingers are extended.

Centuries ago, Native Americans living on the Great Plains found that they needed a common sign language to communicate with each other at large gatherings of different tribes, each with a different language. This sign language included gestures for the numbers one to ten. Your students might enjoy reading and seeing the pictures in Claudia Zaslavsky's book *Count On Your Fingers African Style* (2000), which describes finger counting among five different ethnic groups in various parts of Africa (see also Fig. 7).

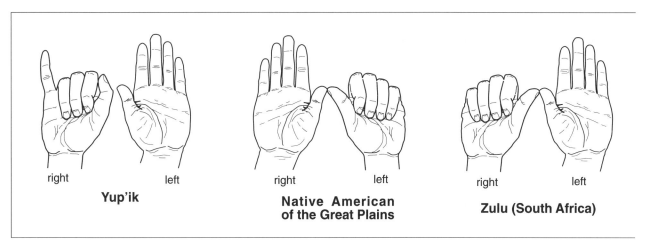

| right | Yup'ik | left | right | Native American of the Great Plains | left | right | Zulu (South Africa) | left |

Adapted from Claudia Zaslavsky, *The Multicultural Math Classroom: Bringing in the World* (published by Heinemann, 1996).

Fig. 7: Different ways of showing the number six (shown from the perspective of the viewer)

History of Math: Numerals and Representing Numbers

The numerals, the written symbols for numbers, used by many people throughout the world originated in India more than 1,000 years ago. Although base ten is used in school, it is not the only base in use in the workplace, in the supermarket, or at the gas station. Where did grouping seconds and minutes in terms of sixties originate? Why do we group eggs in twelves? We use multiple bases in our daily living for different functions. For these reasons, this module challenges students to be flexible thinkers, since they use different ways of grouping and base systems in various situations.

Counting and Grouping in Tens and Twenties:

Base Ten and Base Twenty

The fact that some cultures use only their hands to count, while others use their hands and feet, and yet others only group numbers in sets of two will illustrate to students the diversity of ways of counting, and that counting is a social construction.

People have developed systems of number words. Most European cultures group by tens and powers of ten (10, 100, 1000, and so on). We are accustomed to systems of number words that are based on tens and powers of ten, no doubt derived from people counting with both hands.

However, there are exceptions to base groups of ten. The French word for "eighty" is *quatre vingt,* which means "four groups of twenty." The grouping is twenty, not ten. In other cases, the English language does not always follow the logic one expects. For example, the root "teen," a slight variant of "ten," is added in English to numbers after twelve and before twenty. We do not say oneteen and twoteen after ten and before thirteen. Fourteen means "four and ten," while forty means "four times ten." The English word eleven means "one left" after counting to ten or after taking away a group of ten. Twelve means "two left," after a group of ten is taken away, clear evidence of finger counting using two hands. The idea of something being "left over" after the group of ten is subtracted, which is the meaning of eleven and twelve, is a formation more common to Germanic languages.

Yup'ik number words describe groups of five and twenty. The Yup'ik word for "eighty" means "four twenties," as in French. Systems based on grouping by twenties are also found in Meso-America, for example the Maya, and in West Africa, the Yoruba in Nigeria. In the Mende language of Sierra Leone in West Africa, the word for "twenty" means "a whole person," as in Yup'ik. Although the Mende now count on their fingers, they may have pointed to their toes in the past. Students should start to see that the way a culture names its numbers is suggestive of how its people add, subtract, multiply, and divide.

To increase mathematical understanding of numbers, groupings, and subgroupings, a variety of activities associated with counting in a Yup'ik context are offered. To make the activities authentic for Yup'ik students and those interested in learning about the Yup'ik culture, and to reinforce the connections of the module to Yup'ik culture, Yup'ik words are used to represent important numbers (Fig. 8).

Counting on one hand	Counting on the other hand
1 *atauciq* the pinky on the right hand 2 *malruk* the pinky and the next finger 3 *pingayun* the pinky to the middle finger 4 *cetaman* all the fingers but the thumb 5 *talliman* (one arm) the right hand	6 *arvinlegen* (cross over) little finger on the left hand 7 *malrunlegen* extend the next finger 8 *pingayunlegen* extend the next finger 9 *qulngunritar'aan* (not quite ten) all but the thumb 10 *qula, qulen* (above) thumbs near each other, fingers all outstretched, palms down, extended slightly from the body, at approximately shoulder height. Literal meaning for *qula* is upper half or upper part of the body.
Counting below on one side	**Counting below on the other side**
11 *qula atauciq* traditionally the right foot was advanced and counting begins on the little toe Transliterating the older Yup'ik word for 11, *at-kahk-tok*—it goes down, implying counting continues onto the feet. 12 *qula malruk* add one toe 13 *qula pingayun* add one toe 14 *akmiarunritaraan* add one toe 15 *akimiaq* (the other side) add one toe	16 *akimiaq atuaciq* (one on the other side) counting continues on the other foot and the person steps forward with the left foot. Counting begins on the great toe of the left foot. 17 *akimiaq malruk* 18 *akimiaq pingayun* 19 *yuinaunritar'aan* (not quite twenty) 20 *yuinaq* (the whole person) If the person is sitting he/she extends both hands palm down and extends both feet in front of him/her and says "*yuinaq*." Literal meaning for this word is a "man completed."

Fig. 8: Yup'ik number words, gestures, and literal meanings

Sample Letter

Dear Student and Family:

In mathematics we are starting a series of activities from a module entitled *Going to Egg Island: Adventures in Grouping and Place Values.* Students who have participated in this module have outperformed those students who have used the school's textbook at statistically significant levels. We have found this to be true for both urban and rural classes. Students will also be introduced to an abacus and will learn about the mathematics inherent in Yup'ik culture, geography, and literature, as well as strengthen their knowledge of school mathematics.

Students will group objects in ones, fives, tens, twelves, and twenties by the time they finish this module. One grouping method will be based on Yup'ik ways of organizing quantities, that is in ones, fives and twenties. Another way will be organizing groups into twelves and ones. The arithmetic associated with grouping will include both adding and subtracting, and solving word problems and everyday problems.

Students will explore various ways of representing numbers, relationship among numbers, and place values. They will learn standard ways of adding and subtracting, as well as explore their own ways of creating solutions to adding and subtracting problems. More specifically, they will:

- learn one to one correspondence
- group in fives, tens, and twenties
- use and understand two-digit computation
- demonstrate place value understanding in base 10 and base 20
- use an abacus
- solve problems

The work will be in the context of authentic Yup'ik culture, as described by elders from various places in Southwest Alaska,

This module will enable students to :

- Work in a group and contribute to accomplishing the tasks assigned to the group.
- Use appropriate tools to complete the assignments.
- Organize their own work instead of being told exactly what to do.
- Complete all assignments.
- Produce individual work as well as group projects.
- Demonstrate initiative, creativity and mathematical knowledge.

This module will include information about Yup'ik culture, and the skills that enable the Yup'ik people to survive in the harsh environment of Southwest Alaska.

How can families help?

- Take an interest in the work. Ask your child, "What are you working on in math class?" Or, "How is counting in Yup'ik different from "school" counting?"
- You will find out what they are doing, and your child will learn to put into words what he or she is learning.

Sincerely,

_____, Teacher

Math Goals

By the conclusion of this module, students will be able to perform the following operations with numbers and have the following understanding about numbers, grouping, and place values:

1. One-to-one correspondence

2. Grouping in fives, tens, and twenties

3. Perform one- and two-digit addition and subtraction

4. Use and understand two-digit computational strategies

5. Decompose two-digit numbers into tens and units

6. Demonstrate place value understanding in base ten and base twenty

7. Perform regrouping in base ten and base twenty

8. Use an abacus

9. Solve real-world problems

Introduction and the NCTM Standards

Standard 1:

Number and

Operation

- Understand numbers, ways of representing numbers, relationships among numbers, and number systems
- Understand the meaning of operations and how they relate to each other
- Use computational tools and strategies fluently and estimate appropriately

Source: National Council of Teachers in Mathematics (NCTM). 2000.

Master Materials List

Teacher Provides

Beads (blue and red)
Bundle of sticks (tongue depressors)
Chopsticks
Coins or any uniform objects for the teacher
    demonstration (materials must be different
    than those the students use)
Drums or drum substitutes (coffee cans)
Egg cartons or paper cups
Egg substitutes (washers, pennies, walnuts,
    almonds, marbles, jelly beans, etc.)
Felt pen
Hat
Interlocking cubes (three different colors, ten of
    each color)
Paperclips (two different sizes)
Pieces of foam per tub (from packing boxes,
    unifix cubes, or one-centimeter interlocking
    cubes as substitutes)
Pipe cleaners
Popsicle sticks or twigs (red and green, two
    inches long)
Rubber bands or twist ties
Scissors
Sheet of blank paper
Shoebox or other "bucket"
Sticks
String
Tape
Tea boxes
Twenty sticks for central pile
Washtub or other large container filled with water

Package Includes

CD-ROM, Yup'ik Glossary
Coloring book
Handout, Abacus Worksheet
Handout, Chick Tally
Handout, Circular Bucket Bottom
Handout, Distributing Eggs
Handout, Egg Island Map
Handout, Entire Black-Legged Kittiwake
    Nesting Colony
Handout, Estimate Table

Handout, Estimate Table Two
Handout, Grouping by Twelves and Tens
Handout, Groups of Fives and Ones
Handout, Hands and Feet
Handout, Number of Sticks
Handout, Numbers 10–19
Handout, Playing Cards
Handout, Rectangular Bucket Bottom
Handout, Represent the Eggs as Equations
Handout, Sorting Chart
Handout, Template of an Egg Carton
Handout, Template of a Tea Box
Handout, Twenties, Fives and Ones
    Place Value Chart
Poster, Alaska Map
Poster, Egg Island Map with Grid
Poster, Egg Island Map without Grid
Poster, North America Map
Poster, Using the Body to Count
Story book, *Egg Island*
Transparency, Annie Counting
Transparency, Birds of Egg Island and Their Eggs
Transparency, Chick Tally
Transparency, Egg Island Map
Transparency, Eggs in Groups of Five
Transparency, Estimate Table
Transparency, Estimate Table Two
Transparency, Numbers 10–19
Transparency, Parts of a Sea Bird
Transparency, Portion of the Black-Legged
    Kittiwake Nesting Colony
Transparency, Shapes of the Bucket Bottoms
Transparency, Sorting Eggs
Transparency Template of an Egg carton
Transparency, Tens and Ones Chart
Transparency, The Stone Lady
Transparency, Twelves and Ones Chart
CD-ROM, Annie Playing the Falling Sticks Game
    (Tegurpiit) and Guessing Game *(Kaataaq)*

Master Vocabulary List

Abacus—a counting device.

Bundles—groupings.

Circle—the set of points in a plane that are the same distance from a given point called the circle's center.

Cylinder—a solid figure that includes two parallel bases that are congruent circles.

Cube—a solid figure of three dimensions in which all six sides are equal and all angles are ninety degrees.

Dozen—grouping by twelves.

Estimate—approximating how many, how long, etc.

Grid—a coordinate plane.

Grouping—a way of ordering objects or numbers into distinct patterns.

Place value chart—the position of a number determines its value.

Rectangle—a two-dimensional shape in which opposite sides are equal and all angles are ninety degrees.

Subtraction—the process of finding how many are left when a group is taken away from a set of items.

Two-digit number or a double-digit number—a number from 10 to 99.

Table—a way to organize data.

References

Carpenter, Thomas, Megan Frake, Victoria Jacobs, Elizabeth Fennema, and Susan Empson. 1998. A Longintudinal Study of Invention and Understanding in Children's Multidigit Addition and Subtraction. *Journal of Research in Mathematics Education* 29(1): 3–20.

Cobb, Paul, and Ada Boufi. 1997. Reflective Discourse and Collective Reflection. *Journal for Research in Mathematics Education* 28(3): 258–277.

Fuson, Karen. 1997. Children's Conceptual Structures for Multidigit Numbers and Methods of Multidigit Addition and Subtraction. *Journal for Research in Mathematics Education,* 28(2): 130–162.

Kamii, Constance with Linda Leslie Joseph. 1989. *Young Children Continue to Reinvent Arithmetic: Second Grade Implications of Piaget's Theory.* New York: Teachers College Press.

Liping, Ma. 1999. *Knowing and Teaching Elementary Mathematics.* Mahwah, NJ: Lawrence Erlbaum.

National Council of Teachers of Mathematics. 2000. *Principles and Standards for School Mathematics.* Reston, VA: National Council of Teachers of Mathematics.

National Research Council. 1996. *The Bering Sea Ecosystem.* National Academy Press, Washington, D.C.

Nelson, Edward W. 1899. *The Eskimo About Bering Strait.* Washington, DC: Smithsonian Institution Press.

Piaget, Jean, and A. Szeminska. 1960. *The Child's Conception of Number.* New York: W. W. Norton. (Original work published in 1941).

Secada, Walter. 1996. Urban Students Acquiring English and Learning Mathematics in the Context of Reform. *Urban Education* 30(4): 22–448

Zaslavsky, Claudia. 2000. *Count on Your Fingers African Style.* New York: Writers and Readers Publishing.

Resources

http://www.state.ak.us/local/akpages/FISH.GAME/wildlife/geninfo/educate/awc.htm

This Alaska Department of Fish and Game website has excellent resources on Alaska wildlife and curricular material, including Project Wild. Many links to other sites.

http://www.sf.adfg.state.ak.us/Region2/ie/Teacher_Resources/html/teachres.htm

This is another Alaska Fish and Game website, Alaska Correlations. The hands-on activities are in line with the Alaska State Content Standards. Use this resources guide in lesson planning to address the standards.

http://www.qi-journal.com/abacus.html

http://www.ee.ryerson.ca:8080/~elf/abacus/intro.html

http://www.geocities.com/a1ma_mia/abacus/

Section 1

Getting Ready:

Going to the Island

Activity 1: Covering the Bottom of the Bucket

This module begins with the students listening to chapter 1 of *Egg Island,* a story about a young girl, Jennie, and her cousin, Oscar, who are going to join their relatives on an egg-gathering trip. Jennie is visiting her mother's home village from Fairbanks, Alaska, and does not know what egg gathering is. She has never lived in a village in Alaska. She learns through questions and observations and with help from her cousin.

In this activity, the students follow the action of the story by preparing to go egg gathering and by choosing the bucket that will hold the most eggs. In the process, they engage in the mathematical activities of estimating and counting. Estimating is a common ingredient of Yup'ik life, required in picking berries, hunting caribou, catching salmon, building drying racks, and so on. At the same time, it is an important step in developing number sense because it helps children make the connection between the symbolic representation of numerals and their concrete quantities.

As they practice counting and estimating in this activity, the students are asked to share their strategies with the class in order to emphasize that there are many ways to estimate and count. By having them be creative and invent their own counting and estimating strategies, we are emphasizing a constructionist approach to learning.

Finally, in this activity, there are many opportunities for the teacher to assess the students' level of understanding of the estimating and counting problems they encounter. Assessment at this early stage helps the teacher guide and teach students as they confront increasingly complex estimating, counting, and grouping problems in the rest of the module.

Goals

- To visually estimate the number of "eggs" that will cover the area of different two-dimensional shapes that represent the bottoms of buckets

- To count the number of eggs, or egg substitutes, that cover the bottom of each bucket shape

- To emphasize that there are many ways of approaching and solving a problem

Materials

- Story book, *Egg Island*
- Poster, North America Map
- Poster, Alaska Map
- Poster, Egg Island Map without grid
- Transparency, Egg Island Map
- Transparency, Shapes of the Bucket Bottoms
- Transparency, Estimate Table
- Handout, Egg Island Map (one per pair of students)
- Handout, Circular Bucket Bottom (one per pair of students)
- Handout, Estimate Table (one per pair of students)
- Handout, Rectangular Bucket Bottom (one per pair of students)
- Washers or other round, flat objects such as pennies, plastic eggs (twenty per pair of students)

Duration

Two days.

Vocabulary

Grid—a coordinate plane.

Circle—the set of points in a plane that are the same distance from a given point called the circle's center.

Rectangle—a two-dimensional shape where opposite sides are equal and all angles are 90 degrees.

Cylinder—a solid figure that includes two parallel bases that are congruent circles.

Cube—a solid figure of three dimensions in which all six sides are equal and all angles are 90 degrees.

Preparation

Bring an adequate amount of egg substitutes (washers or other round, flat objects such as pennies or nickels).

Instructions

1. Tell your students you will be reading a story about how some Alaska children get food. Display the maps of North America, Alaska, and Egg Island (without a grid) to help you establish a context for the story. Explain that not everyone wants to go to the store to buy food. In some places, such as rural Alaska, people prefer to hunt or gather their favorite foods. In this case, families will be going out to a special place called Egg Island to collect wild bird eggs (although Egg Island is a fictitious name, the other geographical landmarks and villages mentioned in the story are real).

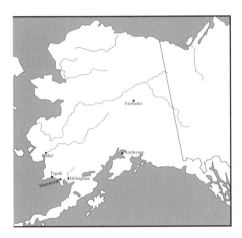   

Fig. 1.1: Alaska map   *Fig. 1.2: North America map*

2. Read chapter 1 in *Egg Island*. Elicit responses from students while you read. For example, "Has anyone here ever gone to visit relatives alone?" "Describe how this may feel." "Have you ever collected foods?" "Describe how you collected wild foods such as berries, mushrooms, or eggs."

3. Place the transparency of the Egg Island map (without a grid) on the projector and ask the students to locate Togiak. Have a few volunteers find these locations—they can come up to the projection screen and point at Togiak.

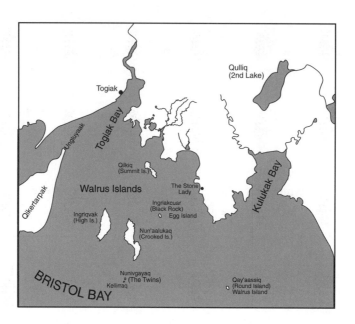

Fig. 1.3: Egg Island map

4. Have the students talk about the way they went about locating Togiak. Locate places in a relational way. (For example: Egg Island is between The Stone Lady and Nun'aalukaq.)

5. Hand out the map of Egg Island (without a grid) to each pair of students. Have students develop a way to find or locate places on the map.

6. Have students discuss and explain how they located their places on the map.

7. If no pair of students comes up with a grid approach then demonstrate for the students by folding the Egg Island map (without grid) in half in one direction and in half in the other direction. Ask the students if this gives them a new idea about how they now might develop a system for locating places. Encourage students to talk about it.

8. Allow students another five to ten minutes to make their system more efficient or to try the paper-folding approach.

9. Ask the students to share their approaches.

10. You can prompt students with the following questions: How many folds or boxes (made by folding) are enough to locate places? Do the units need to be equal?

Part II

1. Tell your students to imagine they need a bucket for egg gathering. When they look around their house, they find two: a cylindrical one and a rectangular prism. Show examples of cylinders and rectangular prisms.

2. Place the transparency of the shapes of the bucket bottoms on the overhead projector and explain that these represent the bucket bottoms. Hold up a washer and explain that it represents an egg. Ask the students to guess how many eggs will fit inside the circle.

Teacher Note

In subsequent lessons when students are locating the characters in the story, have them continue to use and refine their map.

Develop Students' Number Sense

Fig. 1.4: Shapes of the bucket bottoms and washer

3. Place the transparency of the Estimate Table on the overhead projector and mark the range of student guesses in the appropriate box.

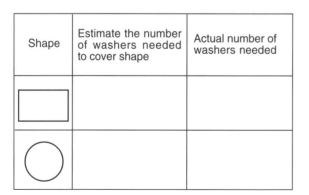

Shape	Estimate the number of washers needed to cover shape	Actual number of washers needed
▭		
◯		

Fig. 1.5: Estimate table

Teacher Note

If this activity is too simple for the students in your class, then vary the size of the object that is to be estimated and have the students see the relationship between size and number. Also, vary the shape and have them determine if the shape affects the number of objects.

Assessment

Circulate around the room and note if any students are having difficulties. Observe if the students understand the Estimate Table—that is, what the symbols stand for, how to read the table, and how to fill it out. Ask each pair how they estimated the number of washers needed to cover the area. Observe and note the ways in which students count, group, and keep track of the washers.

Observe their counting stategies. Washers arranged inside a circle may be difficult to count since there are no definitive starting points, ending points, or pausing points as in a rectangular shape in which the washers are arranged by rows and columns. Do the students start with the outer circle of washers and move inward? Do they start with the central washer and move outward? Do they move each washer outside the circle after they count it to make sure they don't count it a second time?

The rectangle may also be difficult to count since it holds over ten washers. When the students reached ten, did they count on to eleven, or did they start with one again?

4. Have the students work in pairs. Hand out the worksheet of the circular bucket bottom, the washers, and the Estimate Table. Allow about ten minutes to estimate and count the number of washers that cover the shape (the students' shapes are bigger than those used in the demonstration). Encourage students to draw the ways they arranged the washers for counting.

Fig. 1.6: Washers

5. As the students work, observe their estimating strategies. Do they estimate by visually approximating? Or do they estimate by physically approximating, using a body measure?

6. Have the students share their estimating and counting methods, including their illustrations, with the rest of the class to emphasize that there are many ways to approach problems. Ask if the students' estimates were close to the actual counts.

Fig. 1.7   *Fig. 1.8*   *Fig. 1.9*

Washers drawn in a circle, line, and randomly.

7. Repeat steps four to six for the rectangular bucket bottom.

8. Have the students discuss their choice of buckets.

Shapes of Bucket Bottoms

circle   **rectangle**

Estimate Table

Shape	Estimate the number of washers needed to cover shape	Actual number of washers needed
▭		
◯		

Rectangular Bucket Bottom

Circular Bucket Bottom

Egg Island Map

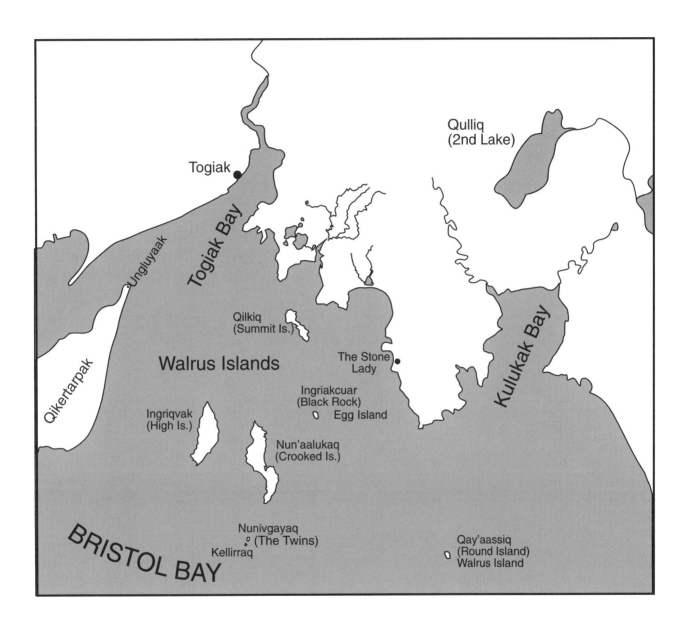

Activity 2:
Estimating Capacity
and Counting Eggs

Students listen to chapter 2 of the story and learn more about the people of Togiak, the surrounding environment, and the different birds and their eggs that inhabit southwest Alaska. Students continue to practice estimating and counting, though this time they are working with three dimensions, the central question being: how many marbles (eggs) fill a tea box (egg bucket)?

To answer this, the students are asked to divide the tea box (or cup) into several layers, estimating and counting the number of marbles (or jellybeans) that fill up each layer. Not only do they continue to develop their number sense by learning to associate estimating with counting, they explore the concept of grouping. Grouping is important for learning how to count large numbers. For example, to better comprehend a large number like eighty, children may see it as eight groups of ten. As in the last activity, students are asked to share their solutions with the rest of the class in order to emphasize that there are multiple ways to approach problems. Teachers are given ample opportunity to assess the students' strategies for estimating and counting in three dimensions, and for grouping.

Goals

- To estimate the number of eggs (marbles) that will fit in the bucket (tea box)

- To count and group the eggs

- To emphasize that there are many ways of approaching and solving a problem

Materials

- Story book, *Egg Island*
- Tea boxes (one per pair of students) or Handout, Template of a Tea Box

- Poster, Egg Island Map without grid
- Pipe cleaner or twelve-inch length of thick string for bucket handle (one per pair of students)
- Handout, Egg Island Map (from Activity 1)
- Tape (one per pair of students)
- Scissors (one per pair of students)
- Egg substitutes (marbles, jelly beans, pennies, washers, etc) (forty per pair of students)
- Coins or any uniform objects for the teacher demonstration (materials must be different than those the students use)
- Transparency, Estimate Table Two
- Handout, Estimate Table Two (one per student)
- Piece of paper (one per student)

Duration

One class period.

Vocabulary

Estimate—approximating how many, how long, etc.
Grouping—a way of ordering objects or numbers into distinct patterns.

Preparation

Bring in enough tea boxes and marbles to supply the student pairs. If you don't have enough marbles, bring pennies or washers or any other object. In the opposite sides of the tea boxes, punch holes, through which the students can insert string or pipe cleaners to make the bucket handles. If there are not enough tea boxes to go around, make enough copies of the tea box template so the students can make one in class.

Instructions

1. Read the next installment of *Egg Island,* chapter 2, "Getting Ready to Go."

2. Have a student mark on their Egg Island map where the characters have travelled.

3. Have the students work in pairs. Distribute the tea box, string or pipe cleaner, tape, and marbles (or anything else that could serve as an egg substitute). If tea boxes are not available, hand out a pair of scissors and the template of the tea box to each pair. Have them cut out the box along the outside dashed lines, then fold along the dark lines. Tape the faces together. Each face has a tab that the student can fold to help tape the box together.

Teacher Note

Observe the students' estimating strategies. Since they are working with volume and dealing with larger numbers (more eggs), they may find estimating more difficult. Do students visually estimate? Do they physically approximate? When estimating the second and third layers, do the students base their estimates on the number of marbles they counted in the first layer?

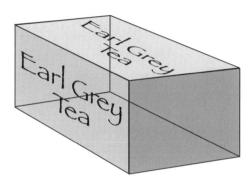

Fig. 2.1: Tea box

4. Tell the students that the tea boxes represent buckets. Have students make a handle for the tea box by inserting the string or pipe cleaner through the premade holes in the box's sides. They can either tie off the string or use tape. For the pipe cleaners, the ends can be hooked up.

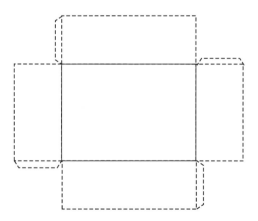

Fig. 2.2: Template of tea box

5. Demonstrate the next part of the exercise for the students by holding up a tea box (representing a bucket) and a washer (or anything else that could represent an egg but that is different than the egg substitutes that the students are using). Ask them to estimate how many washers will cover the bottom of the box.

6. On the transparency of the Estimate Table Two, mark the class range of estimates in the appropriate box.

number of layers	estimated number of eggs	actual number of eggs
One Layer		
Two Layers		
Three Layers		
TOTAL		

Fig. 2.3: Estimate table two

7. Cover the bottom of the box with washers, count them, and mark the number in the transparency of the Estimate Table Two.

8. Tell the students that you want to add a second layer to the first. Have them estimate the number of washers in the second layer. Discuss their estimates. Did they estimate the same number that filled up the bottom layer? Why or why not?

9. Continue to fill the box with a second layer of washers, count them, and mark the number in the transparency of the Estimate Table. Was there a difference in the number of washers between the first and second layers?

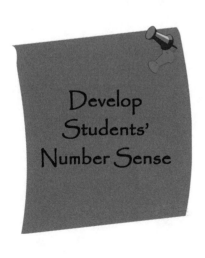

Develop
Students'
Number Sense

One Layer   Two Layers   Three Layers

Fig. 2.4: Bucket and layers

Teacher Note

Observe the students' counting strategies. How do they keep track of the marbles they count? Do they count in groups, say, by twos? When they count the total number of marbles in their tea boxes, do they add the three layers together or do they count every marble in the box again? Do students understand that they are working with groups of objects?

10. Hand out Estimate Table Two and marbles (or jelly beans, if marbles aren't available) to the student pairs. Allow them a few minutes to estimate how many marbles (or jelly beans) would fill the bottom layer of the container. Have them mark this number in the appropriate box in Estimate Table Two. Then, they need to count the actual number and mark this number in the appropriate box in the Table. They need to estimate and count a second layer and finally *three* layers of marbles. At the end of the exercise, they also need to count the total number of marbles in their tea box.

11. Discuss their strategies and answers. Were the students' estimates close to the actual counts?

12. Have the students share their estimating and counting methods with the rest of the class to emphasize that there are many viable ways to approach and solve problems.

13. Hand out a piece of paper to each student and have them illustrate the total number of marbles in their tea boxes. The illustrations may vary. Some students may depict one continuous strand of marbles; some, a clump of marbles; others, an exact replica of the marbles as they were arranged by layers in the tea box.

Fig. 2.5: Drawing marbles in a line

Fig. 2.6: Drawing marbles randomly

Fig. 2.7: Drawing marbles in rows

14. Have the students share their illustrations. Encourage students to talk about different ways of grouping.

Estimate Table Two

number of layers	estimated number of eggs	actual number of eggs
One Layer		
Two Layers		
Three Layers		
TOTAL		

Template of a Tea Box

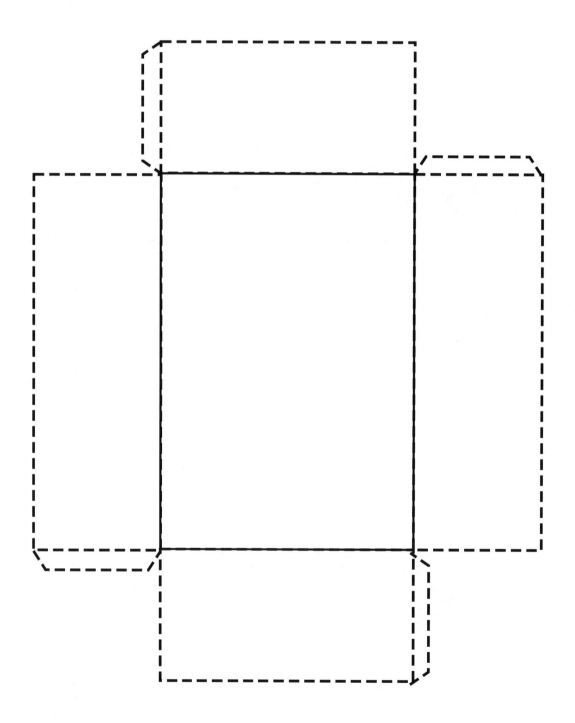

Activity 3:
Grouping Black-Legged Kittiwakes

Students listen to chapter 3 of *Egg Island* and learn about several sea birds that live in the Togiak region: murres, kittiwakes, arctic terns, and puffins. They also learn to distinguish the different bird eggs by their shape, size, and color. The Teacher Note at the end of this activity provides in-depth information on the ecology of seabirds. This lesson is best done as an interdisciplinary one with an emphasis on math and science. Connections to geography are also important here.

As students learn about seabirds, murres, and kittiwakes in particular, they practice grouping in ones, twos, and threes. Small numbers are a good introduction to the concept of grouping, which is the major focus of this module and which is an essential strategy in counting large numbers. Grouping is also important to help students think flexibly about numbers. Objects can be arranged in a variety of ways. For example, a student can take a sum such as 7 and arrange the objects as a set of seven individual ones, or 6 + 1, 5 + 2, and so on. Also, numbers can be decomposed in a variety of ways. In the following activities, methods of grouping become increasingly more advanced until, by the end of the module, students are grouping in fives, tens, twelves, and twenties.

Goals

- To learn about the ecology of sea birds in Bristol Bay

- To count the number of chicks in each nest and the total number of chicks in the colony

- To understand and interpret a table

Materials

- Story book, *Egg Island*
- Poster, Egg Island Map with grid
- Transparency, Birds of Egg Island and Their Eggs
- Transparency, Parts of a Sea Bird
- Transparency, Portion of Black-Legged Kittiwake Nesting Colony
- Transparency, Chick Tally

- Handout, Egg Island Map (from Activity 1)
- Handout, Entire Black-Legged Kittiwake Nesting Colony (one per pair of students)
- Handout, Chick Tally (one per pair of students)

Duration

One class period.

Vocabulary

Table—a way to organize data.

Grouping—a way of ordering objects or numbers into distinct patterns.

Preparation

Read the Teacher Note about the ecology of seabirds in Bristol Bay in preparation for an in-class discussion on this topic.

Resources

http://www.state.ak.us/local/akpages/FISH.GAME/wildlife/geninfo/educate/awc.htm

This Alaska Department of Fish and Game website has excellent resources on Alaska wildlife and curricular material, including Project Wild. Many links to other sites.

http://www.sf.adfg.state.ak.us/Region2/ie/Teacher_Resources/html/teachres.htm

This is another Alaska Department of Fish and Game website, Alaska Correlations. Our hands-on activities are in line with the Alaska State Content Standards. Use this resources guide in lesson planning to address the standards.

Instructions

1. Read chapter 3 from *Egg Island* to your students. Hand out or have the students use their Egg Island maps with grid. Have them locate on their grids the places where the characters travelled.

2. Show the transparency, Birds of Egg Island and Their Eggs.

3. Ask students to describe some of the differences among the types of seabirds.

Fig. 3.1: Murre

4. Ask them to describe some of the differences among their eggs.

5. Show the transparency on the parts of a seabird and discuss these parts with the students.

Fig. 3.2: Glaucous gull

6. Ask the students to share other information that they have about the seabirds. What do they eat? Where do they nest? Why do they nest in large groups, called colonies? How far do they migrate? Supplement the conversation with information from the Teacher Note on Bristol Bay seabird colonies and websites.

7. Tell the students that in the following activity they are going to be biologists, working for the Alaska Department of Fish and Game. They will survey a colony of nesting black-legged kittiwakes to determine whether it is a "good" year for eggs or a "poor" year. Black-legged kittiwakes generally lay zero to three eggs per season, depending on the available nutrient supply. During more productive years, when plankton and small fish are abundant, black-legged kittiwakes tend to lay a greater number of eggs.

Fig. 3.3: Horned puffin

8. To demonstrate the activity for the students, show the transparency of a portion of the black-legged kittiwake nesting colony to the students. Ask the students to look at the nests that hold the most chicks. How many chicks are in those nests? Now ask them to look at the nests that hold the fewest chicks. How many chicks are in those nests?

Fig. 3.4: Black-legged kittiwake

9. Have them count how many nests hold three chicks. Mark this number on the transparency of the chick tally sheet. Repeat for the nests that hold two, one, and zero chicks.

Fig. 3.5: Arctic tern

10. Have students work in pairs. Distribute the handout on the entire black-legged kittiwake nesting colony and the chick tally worksheet to the students. Have them tally up the nests with three, two, one, and zero chicks.

Number of chicks				
Number of nests				

Fig. 3.6: Chick tally worksheet

Teacher Note

The difficulty students have with this activity is understanding that there are four categories of chicks and the number counted for each category may vary. Further, a 1 in the one-chick column has a different meaning than a 1 in the three-chick column. Encourage students to discuss and interpret the table.

Fig. 3.7: Portion of black-legged kittiwake nesting colony

Assessment

Observe and check for understanding. Do your students understand that the numbers in the table reflect groups of chicks? For example, some students misunderstand a "3" placed in the column with 2 chicks. They may not understand that it represents 3 groups of 2 chicks or a total of 6 chicks.

11. Observe their counting strategies. How do they keep track of the nests that have already been counted?

12. Have students report their findings and discuss how they came to their answer. Have the students discuss the chick table and how to interpret it.

13. Have the students discuss the following: What would the Alaska Department of Fish and Game say about their survey of the black-legged kittiwakes? Was it a good year? Bad year? Have the students discuss this and come to a consensus. Encourage students to support their findings.

Teacher Note

Bristol Bay Seabird Colonies

Bristol Bay, located in the southern reaches of the Bering Sea, provides breeding habitat (shelter, food, and water) to an abundance of seabirds each summer. Five of the common summer avian residents are (1) murres, (2) kittiwakes, (3) terns, (4) glaucous-winged gulls, and (5) puffins. These birds migrate back to breeding colonies in Bristol Bay each summer. Some species, like the Arctic tern, travel as far as 12,000 miles (19,300 km), drawn by the rich resources provided by the productive northern summer of plentiful sunlight.

Fig 3.8: A common summer resident of Bristol Bay

The **Bering Sea** is characterized by a shallow ocean depth that rarely exceeds 54 yards (50 m). Ocean currents and storms play an integral role in the productivity of the Bering Sea ecosystem, warming and mixing its water. The Alaska Coastal Current works its way through Prince William Sound and enters the Bering Sea. The current is largely due to fresh water runoff from the coastal mountains and partially driven by wind. It transports relatively warm marine water from the south, through the Aleutian Chain, and onto the continental shelf. An arm of the Alaska Coastal Current also circles counterclockwise through Bristol Bay before continuing northward. The warm water encourages primary productivity which, in turn, propagates through the ecosystem. Turbulence from marine tempests also promotes productivity, stirring up the waters to redistribute nutrients within the ecosystem. Wind and current affect the Bering Sea ecosystem to such an extent that primary productivity can vary as much as 50 percent from year to year, depending on the extent of seasonal storms. This may partially explain why local residents and scientists have observed a vast fluctuation in colony sizes since they began studying seabirds in the Bering Sea in 1970.

The warm nutrient-enriched water, which originates in the vicinity of Unimak Pass and is carried by the currents into Bristol Bay, provides a rich soup to feed **primary production** of marine plankton. The numerous pelagic fish species living in the Bering Sea thrive on this plankton-thickened marine soup. (Pelagic refers to organisms that live in the open ocean or sea, rather than in waters adjacent to land or inland.) In turn, the seabirds, which feed mostly on small fish like capelin, pricklebacks, and sand lance (preying on invertebrates when necessary), flourish during these times of plenty. Conversely, when fish

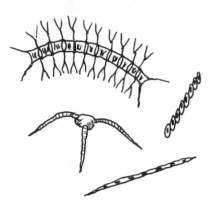

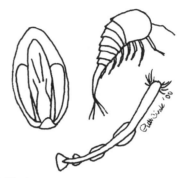

Fig 3.9: Seabirds eat plant plankton   *Fig 3.10: Seabirds eat animal plankton too*

are few, seabirds stop reproducing. Food availability is the primary **limiting factor** to Bering Sea seabird populations.

When food is short, the birds produce fewer eggs or simply do not breed, lacking the nutrients to form eggs and maintain the health of the fledglings. Seabirds most often perish during their first year of life, and those that survive the first winter will live an average of eight to ten years. A seabird doesn't put a lot of energy into incubating an egg and feeding a chick if the conditions for that bird are inhospitable; better to wait until next year.

Another strategy that seabirds have for survival is breeding in large **colonies** located on rocky cliffs, often on islands. The precarious location of the nesting seabirds protects the colony against terrestrial predators, while the sheer number of seabirds living in any one colony dissuades winged predators from ravaging the nests. Each bird species has a preferred nesting location within the colony. Glaucous-winged gulls usually inhabit the higher reaches of a rocky colony, whereas the kittiwakes tend to nest midway up the rock of the colony and prefer locations protected by an overhang. Puffins nest where they can find softer ground to dig out a borrow. Murres seek out the broader rock shelves of a colony as nesting sites.

Seabirds share many **physiological adaptations** to their environment. They maintain **thick feathers** as a waterproof outer layer to stay dry and warm, much as humans wear a raincoat to protect against bad weather. Their **webbed feet** help them maneuver through the water. **Strong, pointed wings** help seabirds on their long migrations and, for some, swimming underwater. Their **sharp, pointed bills** act as hybrid dagger-chopsticks to seize prey, such as fish, from the water. Seabirds are also equipped with special glands that enable them to **drink saltwater** and excrete the extra salt. These shared characteristics enable seabirds to live successfully in the Bering Sea and other marine ecosystems.

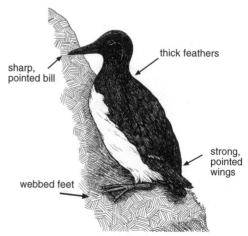

thick feathers

sharp,
pointed bill

strong,
pointed
wings

webbed feet

Fig. 3.11: Parts of a seabird

Teacher Note (continued)

The **murre** (common and thick-billed) is one of the most skilled swimmers found in Bristol Bay, able to dive more than 100 feet (30 m) under water to feed and escape predators. Murres spend eight to nine months at sea. They use their wings to fly under the water, maneuvering more gracefully in the water than the air. Murres have a short tail, so they must use their feet as rudders both in the air and water. In early June, murres lay a single egg directly on rocky cliffs, choosing the broader ledges in colonies when possible. If this egg is destroyed by stormy weather or preyed on, murres are able to lay a second, single egg, or even a third, if enough time remains in the breeding season. Three weeks after hatching, before they can fly, the chicks launch themselves from their nests into the ocean where murres feel most at home. The parents follow close behind.

They perform this acrobatic stunt in the evening in order to escape potential predation by neighboring gulls. After three more weeks, murre chicks are able to fly and, in five years, they will be mature enough to breed.

The **puffin** (horned and tufted) shares the murre's affinity for swimming in the ocean, usually feeding by pursuit-diving to fifty feet below the surface and spending the winter far off shore in the north Pacific Ocean. Puffins are recognized for their colorful beak, which they shed each fall in exchange for a refined, gray version to wear through the winter. Besides attracting a loyal mate, this bright, broad beak equips puffins to hunt efficiently for their young. They can line up numerous small fish crosswise in their

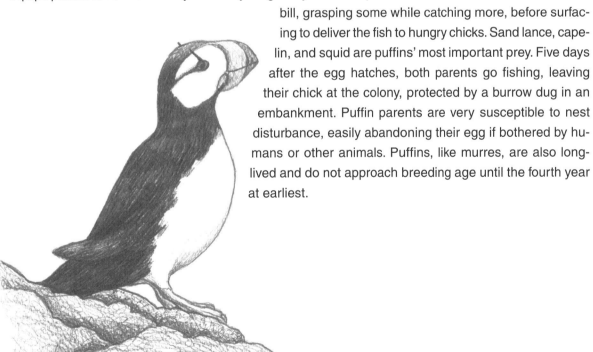

bill, grasping some while catching more, before surfacing to deliver the fish to hungry chicks. Sand lance, capelin, and squid are puffins' most important prey. Five days after the egg hatches, both parents go fishing, leaving their chick at the colony, protected by a burrow dug in an embankment. Puffin parents are very susceptible to nest disturbance, easily abandoning their egg if bothered by humans or other animals. Puffins, like murres, are also long-lived and do not approach breeding age until the fourth year at earliest.

Fig. 3.12: Puffin

Teacher Note (continued)

The **arctic tern** migrates 12,000 miles (19,300 km) from Antarctica to Bristol Bay each spring and returns each fall, for a round-trip of at least 24,000 miles (38,600 km); the most well-traveled bird inhabiting the region. Terns are acrobatic fliers, flapping their wings rapidly, hovering, dipping, and diving. They fly with their bills pointed at a right angle to the water and surface feed on small fish, limiting the amount of

Fig. 3.13: Arctic tern

time spent in the water. Although terns have webbed feet, they feel more at home in the air than on the water, making their long migration across large expanses of ocean all the more incredible. Terns breed in May, usually laying two eggs in a shallow depression on the ground or a cliff ledge. The hatched chicks quickly leave the nest to find camouflage in nearby vegetation. Parents aggressively defend their nests and are known for dive-bombing potential terrestrial predators, such as humans strolling along the beach. Chicks fledge (develop feathers large enough for flight) twenty-three days after hatching, in preparation for the long flight south to sunshine and plentiful food. Young are prepared to breed in three to four years.

The **black-legged kittiwake** is a small pelagic gull. Unlike the other residents of the seabird colonies, kittiwakes make their nests from mud and vegetation on the cliffs. They lay up to three eggs in early to mid-June. It has been well documented that their population size greatly depends on the availability of small pelagic fish, their mainstay. When the fish population is low, kittiwakes will not lay a single egg. Like terns, kittiwakes choose to spend as little time in the water as possible, dipping for fish and occasionally shallow pursuit-diving and surface-seizing.

Fig. 3.14: Black-legged kittiwake

Teacher Note (continued)

The **glaucous-winged gull** is the primary scavenger living in the seabird colony. Gulls are also known to prey on surrounding waterfowl and seabird eggs and chicks. The gull is the "bandit" of the seabird colony, living on what it can scavenge or steal from other birds. Gulls begin breeding at age four. They find nests on sea cliffs in May and usually lay three eggs, depending on food availability. Chicks gradually move to sea to fend for themselves in September and October. As scavengers, gulls are subject to artificial population explosions in response to human development such

Fig. 3.16: Glaucus-winged gull

as canneries and dumps. The supplemental food resource encourages gulls to reproduce in greater numbers. This poses a problem for the other bird species in the colony when the development subsides and the new food source disappears; the gulls then turn to other birds' nests for sustenance.

Reference

National Research Council. 1996. *The Bering Sea Ecosystem.* National Academy Press, Washington, D.C.

Birds of Egg Island and Their Eggs

Horned Puffin

Glaucous-winged Gull

Arctic Tern

Black-legged Kittiwake

Murre

Blackline Master

Parts of a Sea Bird

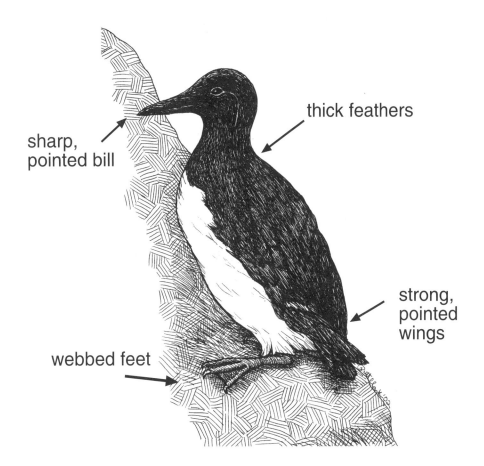

sharp,
pointed bill

thick feathers

strong,
pointed
wings

webbed feet

Portion of Black-Legged Kittiwake Nesting Colony

Entire Black-Legged Kittiwake Nesting Colony

Chick Tally

Number of chicks				
Number of nests				

Activity 4:
Decomposing Single-Digit Numbers: Egg Counters

Today, the class will decompose (break down) single–digit numbers into groups of ones, twos, and threes. By determining if they have all the combinations of a number, students will think about ways of grouping and begin a process of understanding mathematical rules. Does the order of numbers matter, for example 2 + 3 vs. 3 + 2? This exercise prepares students for the following activity, which introduces grouping in fives.

Goals

- To decompose single-digit numbers between five and nine

- To represent the numbers five through nine as addition equations involving the numbers one through three

- To continue practicing grouping in ones, twos, and threes

Materials

- Washers (nine per pair of students)
- Transparency, Eggs in Groups of Five
- Handout, Represent the Eggs as Equations, (one per student)

Duration

Two class periods.

Instructions

1. Have students work in pairs. Distribute the washers (egg substitutes) to each pair of students.

2. Remind the students that previously they were "surveying" Egg Island to estimate the average number of chicks per black-legged kittiwake nest.

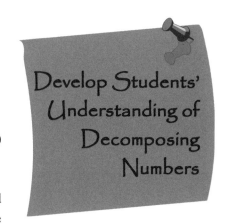

Develop Students' Understanding of Decomposing Numbers

3. Tell your students the following rule: "The number of chicks in each nest is either zero, one, two, or three. Using only the numbers one, two, and three, how many different ways can you combine them to make a group of five?"

4. Demonstrate for the students, first with four objects and group them. Next, have a student come up and group them in another way. Then, using the transparency Eggs in Groups of Five, have them follow along by grouping their own eggs (washers).

5. As you demonstrate, point out that the five eggs arranged in various combinations can be represented as addition equations.

6. Have the students "decompose" six eggs, in the same way that was just demonstrated. Remind them that they can group one, two, or three eggs to make a total of six. (There are seven possible combinations.) Encourage students to decide if they have all possible combinations. If students don't discuss if 3 + 2 and 2 + 3 count as one or two combinations of five, then encourage this as a topic of discussion. If some students discuss it then have them "argue" their point to other students.

7. Hand out the worksheet Representing the Eggs as Equations. Have the students fill out the first box, representing six as addition equations involving the numbers 1, 2, and 3.

8. Have the students arrange their eggs in as many different groupings of one, two, and three as possible, to make a sum of seven, eight, and nine eggs. Have them continue to fill out the worksheet.

9. Observe the students' work. Are they able to come up with all the possible combinations of groups? If not, where do they have trouble? Do they understand the commutative properties of addition equations? Most importantly, have them explain if they have thought of all the combinations.

10. Discuss their strategies to find all combinations.

Math Note

Use this as an opportunity to introduce your students to the rudiments of the commutative properties. For example, ask your students how many ways five items can be grouped or separated. Ask them if the sum of 2 + 3 is different than 3 + 2 (commutative)? Illustrate it in the following manner:

Commutative: 2 + 3 = 3 + 2. Expand with other examples. This property can be applied to larger groupings in future problems and activities.

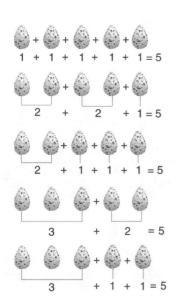

Fig. 4.1: Eggs in groups of one, two, and three

Eggs in Groups of Five

$$1 + 1 + 1 + 1 + 1 = 5$$

$$2 + 2 + 1 = 5$$

$$2 + 1 + 1 + 1 = 5$$

$$3 + 2 = 5$$

$$3 + 1 + 1 = 5$$

Represent the Eggs as Equations

5 Eggs

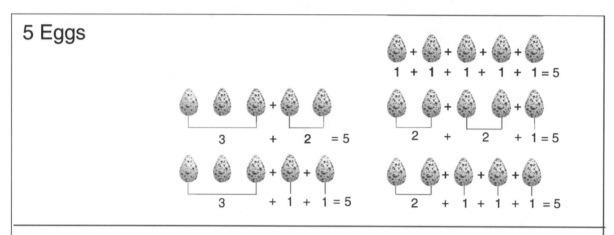

$1 + 1 + 1 + 1 + 1 = 5$

$3 + 2 = 5$

$2 + 2 + 1 = 5$

$3 + 1 + 1 = 5$

$2 + 1 + 1 + 1 = 5$

6 Eggs

7 Eggs

Represent the Eggs as Equations (page 2)

8 Eggs

9 Eggs

Section

Going There:

Going Out into the Bay

Activity 5:
Going Out in the Bay: Visiting the Stone Lady, Grouping in Fives

The class reads chapter 4 of *Egg Island,* in which Jennie and her relatives head out to Egg Island in their boat. En route, they pass the Stone Lady, a rock shaped like a standing woman. Jennie tries to distinguish a face in the rock but can't.

In this activity, students learn about the legend that surrounds the Stone Lady, as told by Annie Blue, an elder from Togiak. They learn a traditional Yup'ik game called Falling Sticks.

The game is then applied to an exercise in which the students learn to group in fives. Grouping by fives is practiced two ways: with sticks and with a worksheet.

Students will continue to work with their personal maps and further their understanding and ability to read maps. Maps are often presented in two forms: (1) a grid with numbers on both axes, for example (3, 2) representing the intersection of 3 on the x axis and 2 on the y axis, or (2) numbers and letters not placed on the grid lines but between them, for example. (3, A) indicating a range. In the latter case order does not matter since (A, 3) and (3, A) are equivalent, while in the former case order does matter. If appropriate for your students, these concepts can be brought up during the map reading portion of the activity.

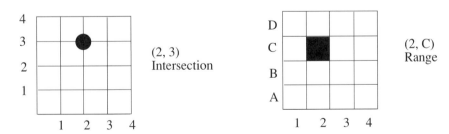

Fig. 5.1: Intersection and range

If time permits, it would be useful and fun for the students to make a petroglyph. Use clay, soap, or flat styrofoam to carve.

Goals

- To add single digits

- To group and bundle (using the game sticks) in fives

- To practice decomposing numbers between one and ten

Materials

- Story book, *Egg Island*
- Transparency, The Stone Lady
- Handout, Egg Island Map (from Activity 1)
- Poster, Egg Island Map without grid
- Popsicle sticks or twigs (twenty three-to-four-inch long for the central pile, five additional for each student)
- Handout, Number of Sticks (one per team)
- Rubber bands (several for each student)
- Handout, Groups of Fives and Ones (one per student)
- CD-ROM, Annie Playing the Falling Sticks Game (optional)

Duration

Two class periods.

Vocabulary

Place value chart—the position of a number determines its value. In this lesson students work in ones and fives.

Bundles—groupings (in this lesson groupings in fives).

Instructions

1. Read chapter 4 of *Egg Island,* and on the Egg Island map, have students point out the route the characters take as they cross the bay, passing the Stone Lady.

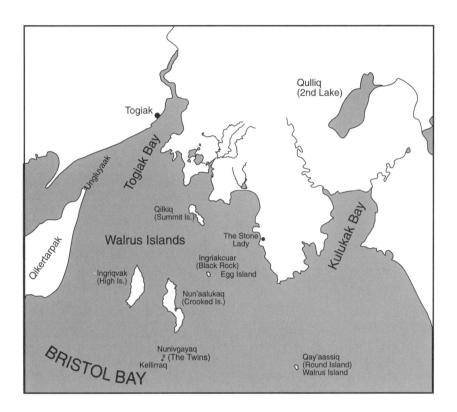

Fig. 5.2: Egg Island map

2. Show the students the transparency of the Stone Lady. Have the students use their personal Egg Island maps to locate the characters and the Stone Lady. Students may continue to revise their maps to make them more useful. Have students share changes that they made to their maps and how they located the characters.

Fig. 5.3: Teacher Nancy Sharp used the floor as a grid system and students recreated the map of Egg Island on it.

Fig. 5.4: The Stone Lady

3. Read the Stone Lady legend on pages 74–75 and have students respond to questions such as, "Have you ever seen any rock formations that resemble people or other things?" "Why was the Stone Lady sad?" "Why did she decide to turn into a rock?"

Demonstration

4. To demonstrate the falling sticks game *(tegurpiit)*, ask for three students to come to the front of the class. Tell the class this game is a traditional Yup'ik game that was frequently played with visitors. The visitor or opponent who comes to defend his group always gets to go first. Optionally, show the video of Annie playing the falling stick game. This is a wonderful video that shows her performing an ancient Yup'ik chant.

5. Place a set of twenty sticks in the middle of the floor, and you and three students should gather around the pile.

Fig. 5.5: Falling sticks for tegurpiit

6. Give each player a bundle of five popsicle sticks or twigs.

7. Hold your right hand flat, the palm facing down, and place all five sticks side by side, across your fingers, as in Fig. 5.6.

Fig. 5.6: Placing sticks on back of hand

8. Toss the sticks off the back of your hand, and try to catch as many of the falling sticks as you can with that same hand.

9. Take as many sticks from the central pile as you caught, and add them to your own pile. For example, if you caught three sticks, take three sticks from the central pile. Explain to your students that normally the game is played with ten sticks across the back of the hand. However, they are playing with five because their hands are smaller than most adults'.

10. Take turns until the sticks from the central pile are gone. Whoever has the most sticks in his or her pile wins.

Math and Teacher Note: Grouping

In this lesson and throughout the rest of the module your students work with regrouping and place values. Regrouping and equal exchanges are important building blocks in developing number sense and, in particular, place values. Further, regrouping prepares students to understand why the procedure in subtraction of borrowing makes sense. For example, when subtracting 9 from 22, you borrow one ten or ten ones from the ten's place. By equal regrouping, 22 now is in the form of one ten plus twelve ones. As students come to understand this convention they will be more able to perform subtraction.

The activities in this lesson begin the process of developing the concept of equal exchanges between a bundle of five and five checks in the ones column. Further, students will also practice decomposing numbers and practice making equal exchanges with double-digit numbers.

In a recent classroom observation, some students were placing their bundles of five in the fives column, some put one check mark for each bundle of five in the fives column, and some put in five individual sticks in the five column. Similarly, in studies by Kamii (1989) and in our own work, many second graders, when asked to represent a double-digit number such as 44 with base ten blocks, often fail to see a difference between the four in the tens place and the four in the ones place. Kamii found that 84 percent of second graders could produce correct double-digit addition, but only 27 percent understood place value.

This confusion is partially about students' developing understanding of place value. They do not quite know that a one in the fives or tens column represents one group of five or ten. Classroom conversation can promote student understanding of place value.

Develop Students' Understanding of Equal Exchange

Thus the activities in this module provide students with concrete experiences in grouping objects in fives, tens, twelves, and twenties. Students represent these groupings within a place-value framework. Classroom conversation is promoted so that students can talk through and represent their contradictory understandings of place value. For example, as they explain and represent the meaning of the fours in the number 44, they begin to further develop their understanding of place value.

Playing the Game

11. Have students get into groups of four and play the game for fifteen to twenty minutes.

12. After they have played, hand out the worksheet Number of Sticks. Have the students fill it out.

13. Tell them that today they will be working with groups of five.

14. Hand out the rubber bands, several to each student. Have them bundle the sticks that they had at the end of the game into groups of five.

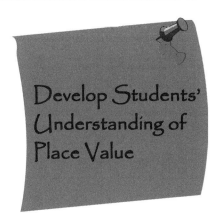

Develop Students' Understanding of Place Value

Fig. 5.7: Students playing and recording

	Sticks at beginning	Number of sticks at end
Player 1		
Player 2		
Player 3		
Player 4		

Fig. 5.8: Number of sticks

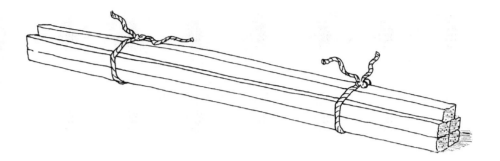

Fig. 5.9: Bundle the sticks into groups of five

15. Ask them to count the number of bundles and the number of individual sticks. For example, if a student ended up with six sticks at the end of the game, he or she would have one bundle of five sticks and one individual stick.

Fig. 5.10: Bundling six sticks

16. Hand out the worksheet Groups of Fives and Ones. Have students put a check in the fives column for each bundle of five sticks they ended up with. Have them put a check in the ones column for each individual stick.

Number:_____

	Fives	**Ones**
1st way		
2nd way		

Fig. 5.11: Groups of fives and ones worksheet

17. Ask the students to represent their final score in another way, this time using only the ones column. If a student ended up with six sticks, for example, he or she would then put six check marks in the ones column.

18. Have students check each other's bundles and fives and ones chart for accuracy.

Math Note

What can the students learn in this activity? Number sense: through using physical materials moving to symbols and ending with numbers. Students should begin to see the patterns. There's only one way of representing numbers 1–4. There are two ways of representing 5–9.

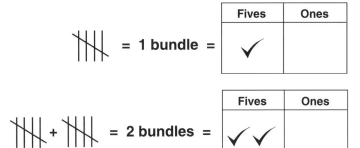

Fives	Ones
✓	

Fives	Ones
✓ ✓	

How many ones are two groups of five?

Fives	Ones

Fig. 5.12: Grouping in fives

19. Have the students represent the numbers 1 through 9 in as many ways as they can, by bundling and by placing checks in the appropriate columns on the chart. Let them explain why there is only one way to represent the numbers 1 to 4. Encourage children to notice any patterns as they fill out the table and have the students explain how they came up with the different representations.

Numbers 1–4	Fives	Ones
		✓
		✓✓
		✓✓✓
		✓✓✓✓

Numbers 5–9	Fives	Ones
	✓	
	✓	✓
	✓	✓✓
	✓	✓✓✓
	✓	✓✓✓✓

Fig. 5.13: Representing the numbers 1–9

An'gaqtar: The Stone Lady

As told by Annie Blue, an elder from Togiak, Alaska, February 1999

Once upon a time when I was a young girl, I heard a story about this married couple. They lived across the bay in a place called Tarunguaq and had a daughter named An'gaqtar.

In time, she [An'gaqtar] married one of the young men who was a good hunter. They became man and wife. As time went on, they had a child.

Around the time their child started walking, her husband mysteriously disappeared. After his disappearance, the wife searched for her husband, but to no avail. When this happened, her husband left for Togiak Lake. The husband's name was Ugli, and he was wearing a hat with a wooden visor. A visor was used when traveling out in the bay to shield from the brightness of the sun.

Finally, as time went by, during her search, she became distraught and eventually lost her mind.

The water in the ocean became hard. As she was approaching old Tarunguaq, she was skipping over the small sea waves. When she arrived at her house, her parents would watch her baby.

On one of her many trips, she came across some children wading in the water. When she came near the children, they became startled and started crying as they scrambled up toward the land, and when they stumbled they became stones.

On her way back home, she started to draw figures on the stone surfaces using her index finger.

Then she molded a human-like figure called Tarunguaq in a place which is now called Tarunguaq. Then again, below them, she made a hollow rock where, when you slap it, the sound echoes back like a rumble.

On one of those days, two boys were making fun of the hollow rock by going to the bathroom in it. Not long afterwards, the two boys who had played around the hollow rock died.

Then again sometime, she made a *qayaq* towing a bearded seal. The bearded seal was complete with feet and a snout. There again, being tired when she arrived, she said, "I am going to become a rock somewhere over there."

She put on her new yearling fur caribou parka and a belt made out of caribou teeth. The belt was cut in half. One half of the belt was tied around her waist, and the other half she used to hold her baby on her back.

Fig. 5.14: Animal figure on a stone surface

An'gaqtar: The Stone Lady (continued)

When the woman first became a stone, the baby behind her back was visible. The belt was also very noticeable. That is how she looked when she left to go to this side of Kulukak *(Quluqaq)*, a place near the Stone Lady.

The stone looks like a human and in front of her is a bowl. When there is going to be a lot of fish, there is a fish swimming in the bowl. One time when there was going to be no fish, the bowl was completely empty.

This is the story as I remember it. I used to see Ugli myself, but I believe that someone has taken him away. Then when an epidemic of great death [flu, influenza] was going to happen, Ugli cried with tears made out of quartz. At the same time, someone heard An'gaqtar's baby making noise. An'gaqtar turned around.

Her human-like statue, called Tarunguaq, which she made, also cried. Everything strange happened before the flu epidemic occurred, in which many of our people died.

So this is the moral of Ugli, that young parents should leave their children at home while hunting.

Today, in a place called Ivruaq, there are some small formations that represent these children just this side of a place called Quluut, on the other side of Nanvarruaq.

Today, the moral that was told is now (still) true about what the ancestors said to the people of then, and to the people of today, and to the future generations to come.

So ends my story. I am Annie Blue of Togiak, Alaska. I was the storyteller.

[NOTE: The story differs from teller to teller and telling to telling.]

Cultural Note

Until fairly recently, Yup'ik was not a written language. Not until the 1950s and 1960s did a writing system for Yup'ik come into today's accepted form. Yup'ik stories were traditionally told to an audience, with the listeners sometimes reminding the teller of certain details and then passing the stories on to others. When an oral story is written down, it may sound brief, incomplete, or even disjointed. If it is originally told in a different language from the one in which it is written, the changes are even greater. Certain expressions, nuances, and even cultural values cannot be conveyed effectively in a translation.

When an oral story is presented as a written one, the audience does not get the benefit of the performance. A performance may lend much feeling and depth to a story that seems lacking in these qualities when written. Tone, voice, gesture, and pauses all contribute to the meaning and emotion of a story. These qualities are not always readily transcribed onto paper. To stress this point to your students, you could take one of their favorite stories or movies and simply paraphrase it. This might help to illustrate what happens to a story when it is presentated in a different medium. Remind your students that telling the summary in a different language might change it even more.

Two Elders Provide Their Interpretation of the Stone Lady

A story may tell us something about a cultural group's philosophy, fears and hopes, rules, and specific ways of behaving. In this particular story, it is important to have some knowledge of the local scene in order to put the story in a meaningful context. The story takes place along Alaska's southwest coast. The weather in this area changes rapidly. These waters are sometimes treacherous due to fog, large tidal influences, rough water, and sea creatures such as sea lions, whales, and walrus. Because of such conditions, danger is ever-present. Thus, living to become an elder is no accident. It depends upon learning from one's elders, carefully observing natural phenomena, and learning from one's experience. The harsh environmental condi-

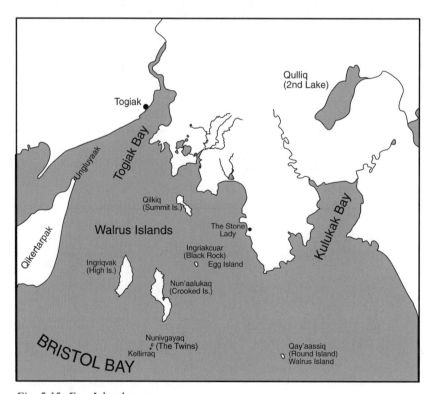

Fig. 5.15: Egg Island map

Cultural Note (continued)

tions and ever-present dangers may look chaotic to the inexperienced traveller but not to the observant person who sees patterns in nature. Listening to elders requires one to learn the rules of living—the shoulds and the should nots. Although the present story may not appear at first glance to be about rules for living, being a keen observer, or listening to knowledgeable others, it is, in fact, about all of this.

The elders and teachers associated with this project were asked, "What does the Stone Lady story mean to you?" Here are some of the things they said: Henry Alakayak, an elder from Manokotak, Alaska, responded as follows:

> *You have to learn how to survive. Like when the water became hard, she walked on top of it. We live by the water and sometimes it becomes very wavy, but you cannot be afraid. People tell us this all of the time. Bad things can happen, but you should not be afraid of it. You have to learn to become a real person and never be afraid to live your life. Because, even when it is windy you are not afraid of death. People might make fun of a person who is frightened of everything.*

The importance of the lessons involved in the story and from the actual "Stone Lady" are reinforced by the importance these elders place on it. For example:

> *This story is almost sacred. Don't make fun of this story or something bad will happen to you. Don't talk about her in a way that people will laugh about it. When you go see her, you don't throw anything at her. Treat her like she's gold. They have stories about what happened to the people that made fun of her. Some people even say that she walks around. She is sacred. I don't know if that is true, but they say that.*

The respect for the Stone Lady is indicative of respect that people have for all living things. This respect for animals is central to living with animals and depending on them for survival. In other stories presented in other modules and elsewhere, it is the animal that gives itself to the hunter. It is the animal who is aware of the care and respect that the hunter shows to living things and thus the animal gives itself. Henry talked about this theme in the Stone Lady story.

> *Everything that you have like this cup right here is like a person.* [This is what he has been hearing since he has been very young.] ... *We treat everything around us like human beings. ... Everything has a "person" (spirit) behind it. That is how he learned to respect everything around him. Like the fish, you bury them in the ground, you respect the bones and skeleton.* [Henry was told this by an old man.] *This has been passed down. They don't know when it was started. The number one rule—respect for all living things. They all have something living behind them. If you don't respect them* ellam Yua *[the great spirit], that* ellam Yua *will do something to you.*

Cultural Note (continued)

In the story An'gaqtar comes upon children wading in the bay. She screams at them. This startles the children and they become stone. At first glance, the possible connections between screaming and becoming stone may not be clear. Henry responds,

> *The children ran away from An'gaqtar when she screamed, the children ran, cried, and fell. They became stone. When she screamed, you could only see their legs when they fell and they became stone. Why did they become stone? Even to this day you don't scare children. If you scare children then their spirit [Yuat]—for example if I scared Isaiah— then his spirit will leave him. A Native person should never never scare children.* Henry said, *You don't scare even an adult. You tap them very softly to get their attention so they won't get startled.*

Mary, another elder, was asked, "What do these stones symbolize?"

> *She startled them by screaming and they became stones. She didn't want them in the water. It is dangerous to be wading in the water and so they can drown by not following the rules. It is not the first time that this has happened and Henry could scream at kids wading in the bay because they can fall in and drown. They symbolize this rule and they are to follow it or else.* [The story is about a specific place where the water runs deep and it is dangerous, sea lions, killer whales, etc.] *Kids don't play in the bay. The children were turned into stone to remind us today that you don't play in the bay.*

Through the story we learn about rules regarding how children should be treated, how parents should act, and that the stones stand as a reminder to the next generation about these lessons.

The elders were asked why An'gaqtar became stone.

> *We have to remember to pass everything down to the next generation. This area is flat and you can still see this figure to this day.*

Henry, just looking at this figure, knows that when he is out hunting he has to be observant, notice things when looking around the area, the land formation, etc., to be a good hunter.

> *The reason she became stone, she wanted to watch the boats go by and watch the people. The people see her all the time. She would be watching us and we would be watching her.*

Cultural Note (continued)

She ended up being good at the end of the story even though she screamed at the children. If we can see her then there is something good ahead of us. When there was going to be a death, things were happening around the village even before it occurred, like the epidemic. Things were happening around the village trying to tell them before that great death [the influenza flu]. These things are noted in the story like [when] the husband cried quartz tears.

Why is the moral of the story about young parents leaving their children at home while hunting?

The moral of the story is that she wants the children left behind because what can happen if they follow someone who goes out to the wilderness? [It would be easy to lose them.] Our mind is very short [ready to go crazy] and sometimes we could lose our mind and become crazy. The mind can be lost because of things like depression, like when you lose a loved one, or you lose your mind. How does losing your mind relate to the children? If you lose your children then it's possible to lose your mind.

The Stone Lady

Number of Sticks

	Sticks at beginning	Number of sticks at end
Player 1		
Player 2		
Player 3		
Player 4		

Groups of Fives and Ones

Number:_____

	Fives	Ones
1st way		
2nd way		

Number:_____

	Fives	Ones
1st way		
2nd way		

Number:_____

	Fives	Ones
1st way		
2nd way		

Number:_____

	Fives	Ones
1st way		
2nd way		

Number:_____

	Fives	Ones
1st way		
2nd way		

Number:_____

	Fives	Ones
1st way		
2nd way		

Number:_____

	Fives	Ones
1st way		
2nd way		

Number:_____

	Fives	Ones
1st way		
2nd way		

Activity 6:
Visiting Annie and Learning About the Old Ways; Grouping in Fives Continued

The class reads chapter 5 in *Egg Island,* in which Jennie and Oscar play a Yup'ik guessing game, called *kaataaq,* and learn a story about this game. The students then play *kaataaq* in this activity and continue to practice grouping in fives and ones. They finish the lesson with a slightly more complicated grouping exercise than that of the previous lesson by representing the numbers 11–20 in groups of five.

Goals

- To learn a Yup'ik guessing game

- To continue grouping in fives while playing a Yup'ik guessing game

Materials

- Story book, *Egg Island*
- Poster, Egg Island Map with grid
- Handout, Egg Island Map (from Activity 1)
- Popsicle sticks or twigs (one red and one green, two inches long) (one of each per pair of students)
- Twenty sticks for central pile
- CD-ROM, Guessing Game *(kaataaq)*
- Rubber bands or twist ties (at least two per student)
- Handout, Numbers 10–19 (one per student)
- Transparency, Numbers 10–19
- Handout, Groups of Fives and Ones (one per student)

Duration

One class period.

Cultural Note on *Kaataaq* game

Players use two small sticks, approximately one to two inches long, for this game. The sticks must be small enough to be hidden in one's closed hand. The green sticks are female and the red sticks are male. The red, or male stick, is called *ui* [husband], and the green, or female stick, is called *tip* [female]. In the game that we played, Annie Blue challenged her opponent by teasing him with a chant.

Instructions

1. Read chapter 5 in *Egg Island*. Discuss the story with your students. Have a volunteer mark on the Egg Island map and grid where the characters have now travelled.

2. Read the Guessing Game story.

Demonstration

3. Demonstrate how to play *kaataaq* by choosing one student to come up to the front of the class.

4. Place twenty sticks in a central pile.

5. Player one takes the red and the green stick and, behind his or her back, switches them from one hand to the next.

Cultural Note: Guessing Game Kaataaq Story

As told by Annie Blue and Mary George, recorded on November 19, 1998 in Fairbanks, Alaska.

There is a story about a man who lost everything in this game. He first lost his material belongings. Then, when he had nothing more, he lost his family members, his wife and children. After he lost everything, he left to a place called *Angvaneq,* and there he played *kaataaq* with a ghost.

He entered (a house) and started to hear some cracking noise in the evening on the ground. This cracking noise was actually someone singing, coming closer as he sang a *kaataaq* song. Then this ghost, who was to be his opponent, came in, and said that he was here to play the game *kaataaq* with him. Whoever loses would be pushed into a crack in the ground, which was between them. So they played, and because the man was playing well against the ghost, the ghost was afraid. When he won, he said to the ghost, "Okay, let me push you now," and when he pushed him, he fell. He could hear the echoes of the ghost's body bouncing on the sides [of the crack]. As soon as the echoes stopped, the crack closed up. He went back and won back all his possessions, including his family, house, elevated cache, kayak, and his other hunting devices. When he was done, he went back to his home with his family.

Fig. 6.1: Kaataaq sticks

6. The player then holds closed hands out in front of him or her, each hand enclosing a stick. Player two chooses a hand and guesses whether it contains a green or red stick.

7. If player two does not guess correctly, player one takes a stick from the central pile and places it in his or her own pile.

8. The procedure continues until player two guesses correctly. Then, player two will hide the sticks behind his or her back and player one guesses. The game is played until the central pile is gone.

9. The player with the most sticks in his or her pile wins.

10. Optional: show the video of Annie Blue playing *kaataaq*. As in the last activity, this video gives an excellent clip of Annie singing an ancient Yup'ik chant, not often heard anymore, while playing the game.

Fig. 6.2: Annie Blue getting ready to hide the sticks

Math Note

As students use the Numbers 10–19 chart, they can see the pattern for constructing numbers between 10–14; these numbers can be constructed in three different ways. For example, the number 14 can be represented in three different ways as follows: fourteen ones; one five and nine ones; and two fives and four ones. Numbers 15–19 can be constructed in four different ways. Also, students can see that on every fifth number there is an exchange as another check is added to the fives column.

Playing and Grouping

11. Allow students fifteen to twenty minutes to play the game.

12. Hand out the rubber bands or twist ties to the students. Have them bundle in groups of five the sticks they ended up with at the end of the game. Have the students put a check in the fives column for each bundle of five sticks and a check in the ones column for each individual stick (on the Fives and Ones worksheet). They will very likely have over ten sticks and so will need to make at least two bundles.

13. As in the previous activity, encourage students to represent their final score in as many ways as possible, using the fives and ones chart.

14. Encourage students to talk about patterns in groupings 1–4, 5–9, 10–14, 15–19. Students should use their work from the previous lesson. Use Numbers 10–19 transparency to show the pattern.

Numbers 10–14	Fives	Ones
	✓✓	
	✓✓	✓
	✓✓	✓✓
	✓✓	✓✓✓
	✓✓	✓✓✓✓

Numbers 15–19	Fives	Ones
	✓✓✓	
	✓✓✓	✓
	✓✓✓	✓✓
	✓✓✓	✓✓✓
	✓✓✓	✓✓✓✓

Fig. 6.3: Representing the numbers 10–19

Numbers 10–19

Numbers 10–14	Fives	Ones

Numbers 15–19	Fives	Ones

Groups of Fives and Ones Worksheet

Number:_____

	Fives	Ones
1st way		
2nd way		

Number:_____

	Fives	Ones
1st way		
2nd way		

Number:_____

	Fives	Ones
1st way		
2nd way		

Number:_____

	Fives	Ones
1st way		
2nd way		

Number:_____

	Fives	Ones
1st way		
2nd way		

Number:_____

	Fives	Ones
1st way		
2nd way		

Number:_____

	Fives	Ones
1st way		
2nd way		

Number:_____

	Fives	Ones
1st way		
2nd way		

Blackline Master

Activity 7:
The Body Counts:
Learning to Count in Yup'ik

Students read chapter 6 in *Egg Island,* in which Annie Blue teaches Jennie how to count in Yup'ik, a system based on the body: one hand means five, two hands mean ten, two hands and a foot means fifteen, and the whole body is twenty. The system is therefore based on fives and twenties.

In the activity, students follow the story's plot by learning to count up to twenty in Yup'ik. This exercise encourages students to think flexibly about numbers, an important step in developing number sense. For example, students learn that the number five can also be thought of as a hand as in Yup'ik body counting, and the Yup'ik word *talliman*, for five, means literally one hand.

Goals

- To learn to count by fives
- To learn some Yup'ik counting words

Materials

- Story book, *Egg Island*
- Poster, Egg Island Map with grid
- Handout, Egg Island Map (from Activity 1)
- Poster, Using the Body to Count
- CD-ROM, Yup'ik Glossary
- Transparency, Annie counting

Duration

One class.

Instructions

1. Read chapter 6 in *Egg Island.* Discuss the story with the students. Ask them if they are familiar with other ways to count, perhaps in a different language. Have them mark on the Egg Island map/grid where the characters have travelled.

2. Display the Using the Body to Count poster. Explain that the Yup'ik have a counting system that is based on the body.

Teacher Note

The base twenty system derives from the natural grouping of digits by five. "Digit" is a Latin word and means "fingers and toes." Digits are associated with counting Arabic numerals, or symbols, from one to ten. They can also be associated with counting objects and numbers from one to twenty, as in the Yup'ik system presented here. This exercise employs four Yup'ik words: *atauciq*, *talliman*, *qula*, and *yuinaq*. These words mean "one," "five," "ten," and "twenty." Literally, they mean "one," "one hand," "above or the top half," and "a complete person."

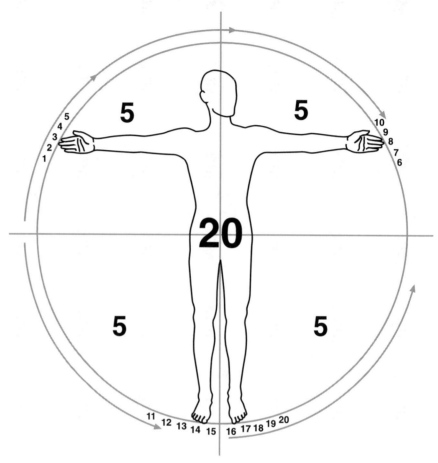

Information gathered from Edward W. Nelson, *The Eskimo About Bering Strait.* 1899, pp. 263–237.

Fig. 7.1: Using the body to count

Counting

3. Review the four Yup'ik words taught in the chapter: *atauciq* (one), *talliman* (five), *qula* (ten), *yuinaq* (twenty). Review their literal meanings: *atuciq* means one; *talliman* means one hand; *qula* means above or top half; *yuinaq* means a complete person.

Fig. 7.3: Annie showing one
as a finger gesture

Yup'ik	Number	Literal	Body
atauciq	one	one	one finger
talliman	five	one	one hand
qula	ten	above	both hands raised
yuinaq	twenty	a person	whole person

Fig. 7.2: Yup'ik words and gestures

Fig. 7.4: Annie counting to six

4. Model how to count to ten. Counting in Yup'ik traditionally begins on the little finger of the right hand and continues toward the thumb. However, ways of counting vary by community and individuals. At six, the crossover number, counting resumes on the little finger of the left hand. When ten, or two hands, is reached, both hands are extended, raised between chest and shoulder height, and moved slightly away from the body, with the thumbs almost touching. Another way to represent ten is to clap both hands together. As you model, show the transparency of Annie counting to ten.

5. Count to ten and have students follow along.

Fig. 7.5: Annie showing ten

6. Model how to count from eleven to twenty. To display eleven, extend both hands in front of you, palms out, or clap hands together, then point to the little toe of the right foot. Counting continues along the right foot to the big toe, which represents fifteen. At sixteen, the Yup'ik word means "it goes over," and you must point to the large toe of the left foot. This continues until the small left toe is reached. (This custom may vary.)

7. To display twenty (a person complete), extend both hands, palms down, and tap feet together. Another way some teachers and students represent twenty is to clap your hands together, then tap your feet. (This is especially useful for school children).

8. Count from eleven to twenty and have the students follow along.

9. Play "Annie Says" (a game just like "Simon Says"). Call out the numbers from one to twenty and have students display the number with hand gestures.

10. If you want, call out the Yup'ik words that the class has learned: *atauciq, talliman, qula,* and *yuinaq.* Have them repeat the words after you as they make the appropriate body gestures.

11. Show Yup'ik glossary of Annie counting in Yup'ik.

12. If time permits, provide a few simple oral math problems in Yup'ik. Use the CD-ROM and the Yup'ik numbers to help the students. For example, *qula + qula = ?; talliman + atauciq =?; talliman + qula = ?.* Students can make up some problems as well.

Annie Counting

Annie Blue Counts 1.

Annie Blue Counts 6.

Annie Blue Counts 9.

Annie Blue Shows 10.

Activity 8:
Regrouping by Exchanging

In this lesson, students learn to group in quantities of twenty, adding to their knowledge of grouping in quantities of fives and ones. They also learn about "exchanging," i.e., five ones for one five, four fives for one twenty. The concept of exchanging is an important milestone for students as they learn how to add and subtract. Exchanging includes the concept of equal value. Students continue to practice Yup'ik words and body gestures, thus furthering their abilities to think flexibly about numbers. It is important for students to understand that exchange includes the concept of equal value. Also, this lesson emphasizes the most efficient way to construct or group quantities. In the previous lesson students explored multiple ways to group quantities.

Goals

- Efficient grouping strategies fives and twenties
- Learning how to make exchanges of equal value

Materials

- Bundle of sticks (tongue depressors) (twenty per student)
- Rubber bands or twist ties (four per student)
- Handout, Twenties, Fives and Ones Chart (enlarged to fit 11x14 paper) (one per student)
- Handout, Hands and Feet (one per pair of students)
- Scissors (one pair per pair of students)

Vocabulary

Grouping—a way of ordering objects in ones, fives, and twenties

Instructions

1. Hand out the sticks and rubber bands or twist ties to each student.

2. Hand out the twenties, fives, and ones chart. Ask the students to describe a difference in this chart compared to the one they've been using in the previous exercises. They should note that this chart has a new column, the twenties column.

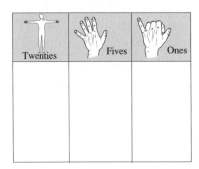

Fig. 8.1: Twenties, fives, and ones chart

3. Remind students that the Yup'ik system of counting is based on ones (one finger), fives (hands and feet), and twenties (a person complete). Have them bundle the twenty sticks into groups of five. They should have four groups of five sticks.

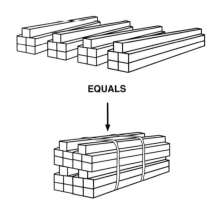

Fig. 8.2: Exchanging bundles

Fig. 8.3: Elders (l to r) John Pauk, Joshua Philip, Henry Alakayak, Sam Ivan, and Mary George group sticks in bundles of five.

4. Call out various numbers between one and twenty (in English) and have the students represent these numbers by bundling and by checking the appropriate columns in their charts. Tell them they must *use the fewest bundles and checks possible* (this is a new concept for them; in previous exercises, they were supposed to determine all the possible combinations). For example, in this exercise, to represent fif-

teen using the least amount of checks, students should put three checks in the fives column and disregard the two other ways to represent the same number.

5. Repeat step #4, only this time call out the numbers in Yup'ik and/or make Yup'ik body gestures.

6. Explain the concept of exchanging: a five-dollar bill can be exchanged for five ones or a twenty-dollar bill can be exchanged for four fives. Explain that what they have been doing during the last few exercises, (bundling sticks into groups of five and putting checkmarks in the appropriate columns of the fives and ones chart), is a form of exchange. Ask the students: "How many bundles of five sticks would you need to trade for two "hands?" "How many for three hands?"

7. Have students work in pairs and hand out the scissors and Hands and Feet worksheet.

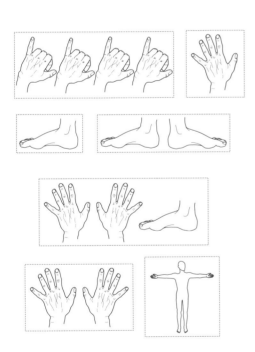

Fig. 8.4: Hands and Feet

8. Have them cut out the squares and rectangles of hands, feet, and the whole body.

9. Have one student hold up one of the cutouts from the worksheet or a combination of cutouts while the other student represents that number by bundling his/her sticks and then by checking the appropriate columns in the twenties, fives, and ones chart. Have students continue like this for five or ten minutes, or assign numbers and have the students make these numbers using the cutouts. Emphasize again that they need to use the fewest bundles and checkmarks possible. Ask students to describe their strategies for grouping.

10. To conclude, ask students to discuss the following:

    Can you exchange

    a. a "foot" for a "hand"?

    b. four "feet" for a person?

    c. six fingers for what?

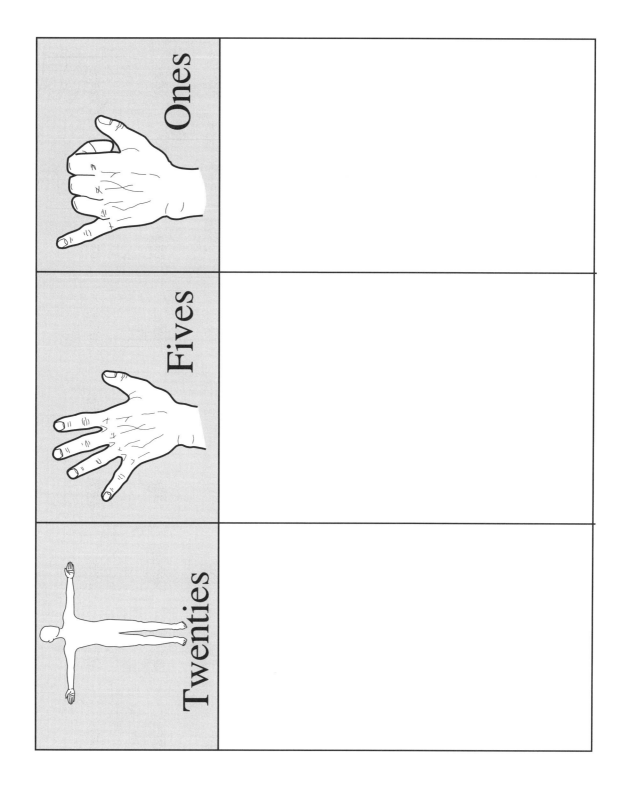

Twenties, Fives, and Ones Place Value Chart

Hands and Feet

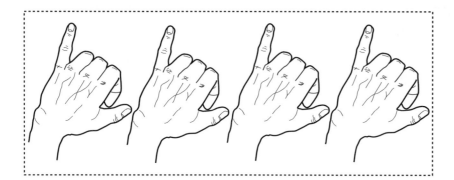
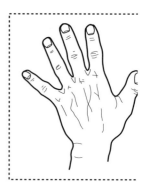
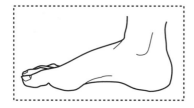
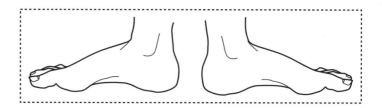
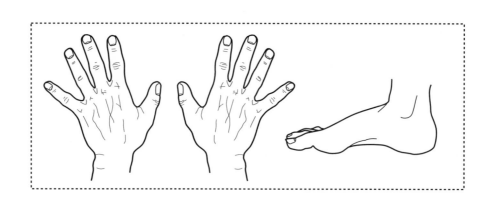
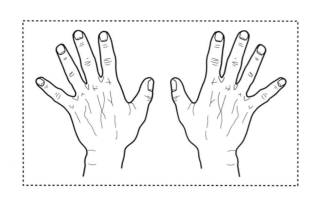
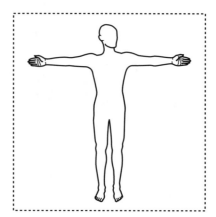

Activity 9:
Introducing the Abacus:
A Counter to Twenty

In today's story, *Egg Island* chapter 7, Jennie and Oscar talk about different abaci. (See Activity 10 for instructions on how to make your own Yup'ik abacus.)

The Yup'ik numbers one through five are constructed in an additive manner; one more is added to the last number until five is reached. The second grouping of fives is additive through number eight. Nine is a subtractive construction—one less than ten, or not quite ten. Eleven through fifteen, and sixteen through eighteen are again additive, but nineteen is subtractive; not quite a whole person. Ten represents a midpoint, literally the "top half of a person."

Goals

The students will be introduced to a type of abacus, developed specifically for this project and based on the Yup'ik body-related system of ones, fives, and twenties. Different ways of representing numbers and groupings are the major math concepts developed in this activity.

- To introduce a counting device (abacus) to the students

- To use the abacus to form numbers up to twenty

- To reinforce and further student's understanding of equal exchanges

- To represent numbers in multiple ways; on the abacus, with the body, and by using bundles and individual sticks

- To estimate a number and verify the accuracy of the estimate

Materials

- Poster, Egg Island Map with grid
- Story book, *Egg Island*
- Yup'ik abacus from activity ten

Math Note

The concept of matching, or one-to-one correspondence, is essential to numeration and the counting process. In some Yup'ik traditions, the digits of the hands and feet are employed as counters up to twenty. The fingers and toes illustrate a concrete, one-to-one correspondence with whatever is counted.

Matching objects to toes and fingers facilitates the idea of recursion; each number in a sequence is the previous number plus one. After matching is understood, fingers and toes come to represent, or stand apart from, the actual item counted.

This understanding allows people to consider numbers apart from the objects that they represent and makes counting a transportable, easy, and abstract tool.

Teacher Note

Let the students develop and explain the concept of "exchanging" in which number groupings are reconfigured. Have students explain their methods to other students who may not quite understand the concept of exchanging on the abacus.

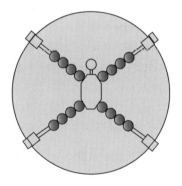

Fig. 9.1: Zero position

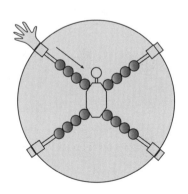

Fig. 9.2: Five

Duration

Two class periods.

Vocabulary

Abacus—a counting device

Preparation

Make a Yup'ik abacus.

Instructions

1. Display the map poster and read today's section of *Egg Island,* chapter 7, "A Yup'ik Abacus." Information from this chapter will also be relevant for the next two activities.

2. Ask the students if they have ever used an abacus.

3. Have students gather around you and show them the Yup'ik abacus. Ask for one student to be a "human abacus." Ask the student to take off his or her shoes and socks, or use the clapping method for counting described in Activity 7, and to stand next to you while you hold the Yup'ik abacus.

4. Show the abacus in its zero position.

5. Begin counting. Have the student hold his right arm out to the side at shoulder height, fist closed. On the left side of the abacus, move one bead toward the folded down hand.

6. While you are moving the bead toward the hand, the student will extend only the pinky finger.

7. Continue this process, until all beads on the left side are moved toward the hand and the student has all four fingers extended.

8. Turn out the hand on the left side of the abacus, and have the student unfold his thumb. This is five.

9. Have the student remain as five and move the abacus beads back to the center. Ask your students, "Which bead will be shown when six is formed?" Demonstrate by moving one bead on the right side of the abacus toward the hand. The human abacus (the student) should demonstrate by extending the pinkie finger of his or her left hand.

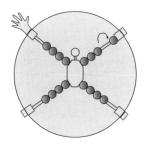

Fig. 9.3: Six

10. Continue this process until ten is reached, then move the beads back to the center and flip out the hand on the right side of the abacus. The student holds out her left hand, thumb extended.

11. Now ask, "What should we do to make eleven on the abacus?" Move one bead toward the foot on the left side of the abacus.

12. Have your student extend the right foot and point to his small toe, or if he doesn't wish to remove his shoes, he can clap and extend his fingers to represent the teens.

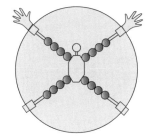

Fig. 9.4: Ten

13. Continue the process to twenty.

14. At twenty, have the student stretch out both hands and feet. Tell the class: "In the Yup'ik Eskimo system, this is 'one person complete.' We call it 'twenty.'"

15. Review by calling out various numbers. Have some students show them on your abacus and others with their bodies.

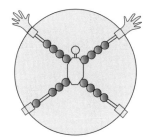

Fig. 9.5: Eleven

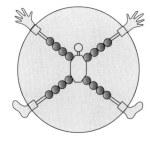

Fig. 9.6: Twenty

Activity 10:
Making an Abacus

The introduction of the abacus provides students with another method for calculating and/or performing basic operations. Practice with the abacus should also strengthen their sense of numbers, particularly since the abacus used in this module is based on the Yup'ik system of counting and organizing numbers.

The following activity challenges your students to further their understanding of grouping, exchange, and place values. They exchange four beads and push them back toward the center (as an operation that equals the fifth bead) and then exchange it for one hand. This exchange is repeated for the sub-groups of the other hand and each foot. After nineteen, twenty beads are exchanged for a whole person, or a unit of twenty. For those students who require a further challenge have them decide the construction of the abacus. For example, ask students if the abacus should have four or five beads for each sub-group. Please note that the Japanese four-bead abacus works similar to the Yup'ik abacus developed for this module, while the Chinese abacus has five beads. This challenge will have the students thinking about exchange and number representation. Their logic and thinking about this will provide valuable information about their understanding of place value.

Goal

- To make a Yup'ik base 20 abacus

Materials

- Pipe cleaners (two per student)
- Sixteen blue and four red beads for each student
- Handout from Activity 8, Hands and Feet

Preparation

Please read the teacher note about the abacus on pages 112–114.

Instructions

1. Hand out the beads and pipe cleaners.

2. Have the students lay their pipe cleaners on their desks in an X formation.

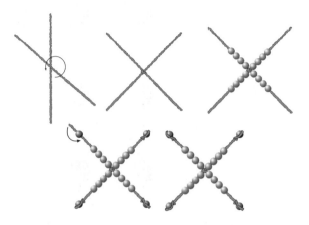

Fig. 10.1: How to make an abacus

Develop Students' Understanding of Equal Exchange

3. Have them turn down the upper right "arm" of the X, and at the same time turn up the lower left "leg" of the X, thus making a knot tying one leg of the abacus to the other.

4. Challenge the students to discuss within their small groups (three students) if there should be four beads or five beads per section of the abacus. Have the students discuss the reasons why the abacus should or should not have four or five beads. After students have had a chance to talk about this, have students in each group explain their choice of four or five beads. Have the students make their abaci.

5. Have them take one red bead and string it onto the end of the left "arm," pushing it down about one inch.

6. Pull the end of the pipe cleaner around the bead and twist the pipe cleaner around itself so it loops around the bead.

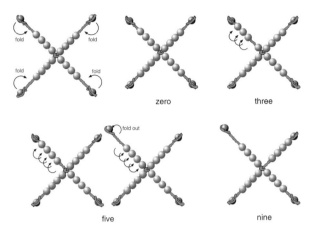

Fig. 10.2: How to display numbers zero through nine

7. Repeat this procedure for the right "arm" and both "legs."

8. The red beads (hands or feet) can be turned down, then turned back up to represent five, ten, fifteen, and twenty.

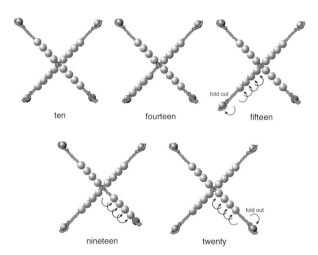

Fig. 10.3: How to display numbers ten through twenty

9. Practice. Use the Hands and Feet material that was used previously in Activity 8. Display one hand and have students represent it on their abacus. Display two hands. Again have students represent it on their abacus. Display any number of combinations of the hands and feet cutouts (as long as they don't add up to more than twenty) while the students represent the numbers on their abaci.

Activity 11:
Practice with a Yup'ik Abacus

The following activities are intended for those first grade and second grade students who need further mathematical challenges and practice in using the Yup'ik abacus, including representing and manipulating numbers up to 20. There are also some problems for second graders that involve numbers greater than twenty.

In this module, two-digit numbers on the Yup'ik abacus are associated with various body positions (digits, hands, feet). This will help students move from concrete notions of quantity to more abstract quantities, as represented on the abacus.

The Yup'ik counting numbers support students' understanding of grouping and decomposing numbers because the Yup'ik system of counting is an additive system of groups of twenties, fives, and ones. Students will become aware of how numbers are constructed. For example, for numbers 20 or higher, you typically have the following construction for a number such as 73: $20 + 20 + 20 + 10 + 3$. [*Yuinaat pingayun* (3 twenties) *qula* (10) *pingayunek cipluku* (with 3 left over)].

To reinforce the concept of place value, make the following and place on the floor: a large picture of a person and the value twenty, a hand and the value five, and a finger and the value of one. Call out a number and have students determine how to construct that number by deciding how many students need to stand in the twenties place, the fives place, and ones place. Ask another group of students to construct that number in another way. These physical experiences associating grouping and place value may provide them with the experiences necessary to make the conceptual leap to understanding place value.

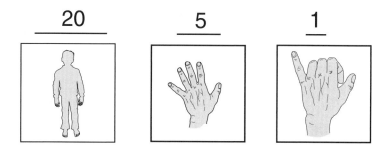

Fig. 11.1: A person, a hand, a finger

Goals

• To use the Yup'ik abacus to construct numbers greater than 20

• To use the Yup'ik abacus to add and subtract double-digit numbers

The Yup'ik abacus included in this part of the module can be used for addition and subtraction, and it allows students to represent numbers up to 20 on to 100, depending on which abacus is used. It allows them to form numbers in two ways: by adding through a cumulative process, or by subtracting. Having students note how they represent a number connects both constructivist approaches to adding and subtracting, as well as more conventional paper and pencil. Practice!

Materials

• Story book, *Egg Island*
• Poster, Egg Island Map with grid
• Handout, Egg Island Map (from Activity 1)
• Yup'ik abacus from Activity 10 that students made (one for each student)

Instructions

1. Read *Egg Island,* chapter 8.

2. Show the children the poster of Egg Island with grid and mark on the map where they have travelled. Students may continue to note the characters' travels on their maps.

3. Have the students work in pairs. Hand out an abacus to each student.

4. Call out numbers between 1 and 20, and have students, one at a time, demonstrate the number on their abacus.

5. Provide additional practice for your students. Have them pair up, using two abaci between them, as they explore numbers greater than 20. Have them show the following numbers on their abaci: 20, 25, 29, and 36.

Fig. 11.2: Students using abacus

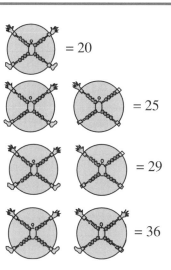

Fig. 11.3: Displaying the numbers 20, 25, 29, 36

6. Have the students solve the following problems using their abaci. Students should work in pairs. Most importantly, have students explain their process of solving to their partner. Circulate around the room and ask students to show and explain how they solve these problems. Pay attention to their process of exchanging. Have a few students at the end share their strategies with the class.

    a. 3 + 3 =
    b. 12 – 4 =
    c. 13 + 6 =
    d. 19 + 7 =
    e. 26 – 5 =
    f. 20 – 6 =
    g. 23 – 19 =

Teacher Note

The Abacus[1]

The abacus has been in existence for at least 2500 years, and aids in counting and performing basic arithmetic operations (addition, subtraction, multiplication, and division). Although today the abacus is associated primarily with China, Japan, and Russia, where it is commonly used, its origin may be with the Greeks, Romans, or ancient Babylonians. The Greek word *abax* means "calculating board," or "calculating table." One of the earliest surviving (abacus) counting boards is the Salamis tablet, used by the Babylonians circa 300 BC and discovered in 1899 on the island of Salamis. The first Roman abaci were probably sandboxes. Markings would have been made with a person's finger and erased after the calculation was agreed upon. There is also evidence that a type of abacus existed in Peru. Furthermore, in ancient Peru the Quipu used to record data. Yupana (an abacus) was used to calculate numbers. The Chinese abacus is shown below.

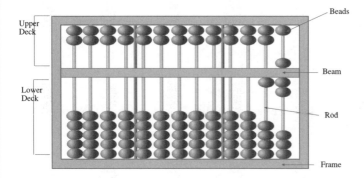

Fig. 11.4: Chinese abacus

As the abacus developed over time, it took the form shown below, which is a Japanese abacus.

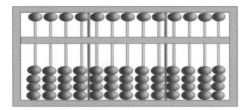

Fig. 11.5: Japanese abacus

The Japanese abacus, called the *soroban*, is an adaptation of the Chinese abacus, or *suan pan*. However, the *soroban* is more efficient in that fewer beads need to be moved. Each vertical strand has four beads below the crossbar, and one bead above it.

1. The following sources were used to develop this teacher note: http://www.qi-journal.com/abacus.html, http://www.ee.ryerson.ca:8080/~elf/abacus/intro.html, http://www.geocities.com/alma_mia/abacus/

Instructions for Reading the Chinese Abacus—*Suan Pan*

To show 5 on the *suan pan*, the Chinese abacus, push five beads up to the crossbar, then push them down, and push one of the two beads above down to the crossbar. This is an exchange, or trade, of five separate units for a single bead representing 5. Similarly, to show 10, you push the five lower beads up to the crossbar and one upper bead down to the crossbar, then exchange the five below for the second bead above. Next, exchange the two upper beads for one lower bead in the strand to the left. In other words, the Chinese abacus allows for three different ways to show 10.

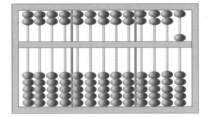
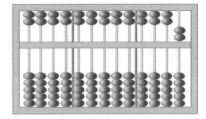

Fig. 11.6: Chinese abacus showing 5.   *Fig. 11.7: Chinese Abacus showing 10.*

Instructions for Reading the Japanese Abacus—*Soroban*

The Japanese abacus, the *soroban,* allows only one way to show 5 and one way to show 10. It operates on a cumulative principle.

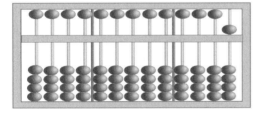
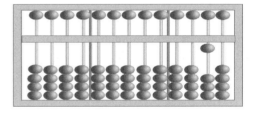

Fig. 11.8: Japanese abacus showing 5   *Fig. 11.9: Japanese abacus showing 10*

The example below shows 4 on the Japanese *soroban.*

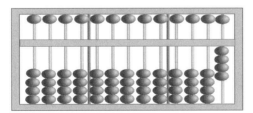

Fig. 11.10: Japanese abacus showing 4

Teacher Note (continued)

The **Yup'ik abacus** also operates on a cumulative principle. Each strand, or "arm" or "leg," has four beads. To represent 5 on that strand, you extend the "hand" ("foot") at the end of the strand.

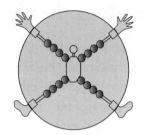

Fig. 11.11: Yup'ik abacus showing 20

The Yup'ik abacus to one hundred, developed for this project, operates on the cumulative principle. It can represent numbers from 1 to 100. Each "person" represents 20, thus five "people" equals 100. However, unlike the Japanese and Chinese abacus, there are many ways to represent units 4 or less. For example, if every bead is worth one unit, then 4 can be constructed by pushing four beads to the left towards an arm or a leg. Similarly, one bead from each strand can be pushed toward the hands and foot, forming 4. Using the abacus this way provides students with an opportunity to deconstruct numbers and make equal exchanges.

Fig. 11.12: Yup'ik abacus to 100

Its function is to assist students in counting and grouping, and for students to become flexible thinkers. The abacus allows children to count to twenty. However, the second and more sophisticated abacus of this module allows children to count to 399, and to perform arithmetic operations to 399. Both abaci are structured from the existing Chinese and Japanese abaci, and adapted to the way that the Yup'ik language structures numbers, that is in groups of ones, fives, and twenties.

Section

On the Island

3

Activity 12:
Oral, Written, Bundles, Finger Gesture, and Numbers Displayed on the Abacus: A Game and Optional Activity

Use this activity if students need to associate oral and written forms of numbers and need more practice with displaying numbers in various forms. This game-like format provides students with an opportunity to connect numbers in their oral and written forms and to display them concretely with their digits and on an abacus. The game includes five decks of cards, each showing numbers differently: on an abacus, as a finger gesture, as a written numeral, as a spoken word, or as a bundle. Students will draw a card from one of the decks, then display the number in one of the multiple ways just described: as a finger gesture, on an abacus, as a written numeral, as a spoken word, or as a bundle, depending from which deck the card was drawn.

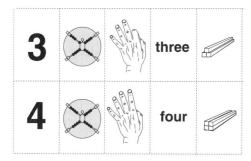

Fig. 12.1: Game card

Students can play variations of the game as well. One variation uses subtraction. A student draws a number, then displays the additional number needed to make the sum of 10 (or 20). Another variation uses addition. A student draws a number, then displays the number made when 10 (or 20) is added to it.

Goals

- Making sums of 10 and 20 with addition

- Subtracting numbers from 10 and 20

- Representing numbers in various forms

- Connecting written and oral numbers to finger gestures, bundles, and display on an abacus

- Improving students' accuracy and speed in performing mental arithmetic to 10 (and 20)

Materials

- Scissors (one per group of five students)
- Handouts, Playing Cards (one set per group of five students)
- Yup'ik abacus from Activity 10 that students made (one per student)
- Sticks (twenty per group of five students)
- Rubber bands or twist ties (one per student)

Vocabulary

Subtraction—the process of finding how many are left when a group is taken away from a set of items.

Preparation

Copy enough game cards for the students to cut out. There should be one set of cards per group of five students.

Instructions for Playing the Game

1. Have students get into groups of five. Hand out a pair of scissors and a set of game cards to each group. Have them cut out the cards and shuffle the cards into one deck.

2. Hand out an abacus, twenty sticks, and four rubber bands or twist ties to each group.

3. One student picks a card from the deck and displays the number as it is represented on the card. For example, if the card says, "three," the student simply says the number out loud. If the card has a finger gesture, the student makes that gesture.

4. The remaining students go around in a circle, and each one displays the same number in one of the other ways the number is represented on the cards. So after the first player has said "three," another player must write the number 3 down; another player must make the Yup'ik hand gesture for 3; another player must show 3 on the abacus; and the final person must express 3 as a bundle. Since the sticks are bundled into groups of five, any number less than 5 does not require bundling. Only the correct number of sticks must be shown.

5. After the number has been represented five ways by the group, the next player draws a card from the deck.

6. Have the students play for approximately ten minutes.

Variation One

1. The first student picks a card from a deck, then displays the additional number needed to make the sum of 10 (or 20). The student must display the answer in the manner depicted on the card. So, for example, if a player picked the card of the abacus reading 3, he or she would need to display the number 7 on his or her abacus. In this variation, there is no need for the other players to display the number 7 in the four other possible ways; their job is to check the student's subtraction.

2. The next player chooses a card from the deck, and the game continues until all players have had at least three chances to draw from the deck.

Variation Two

1. The first student picks a card from a deck, adds 10 to that number, then displays the sum in the manner depicted on the card. So, for example, if the card with the hand gesture showing the number four was drawn, the person would need to add 10 to 4 and make the Yup'ik sign for 14. As in variation one, the other players' job is to check the student's addition.

2. The game continues as in variation one.

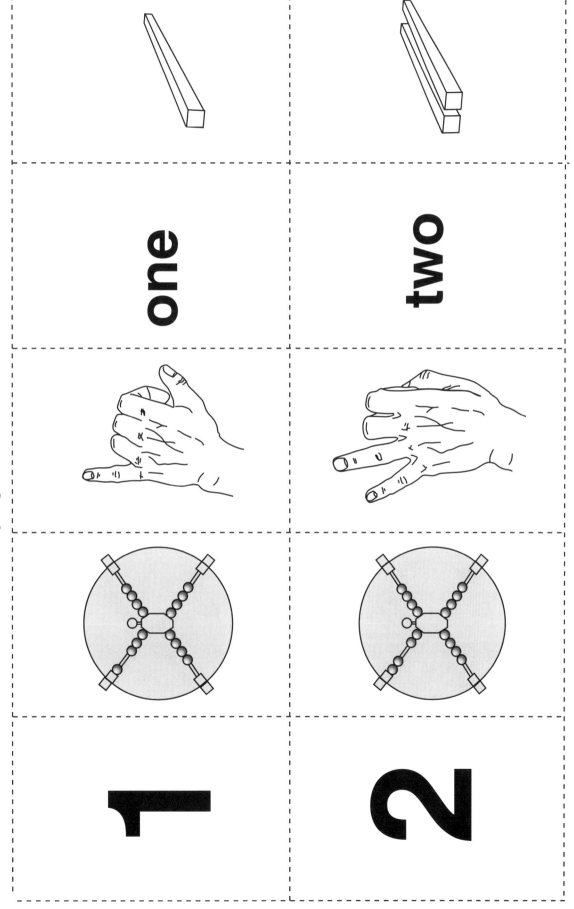

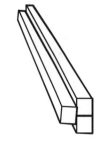
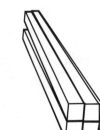

three

four

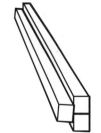
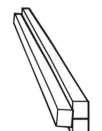
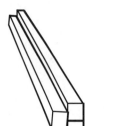
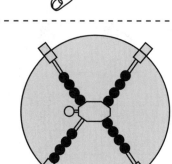
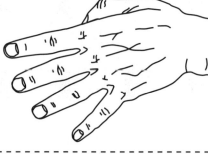

3

4

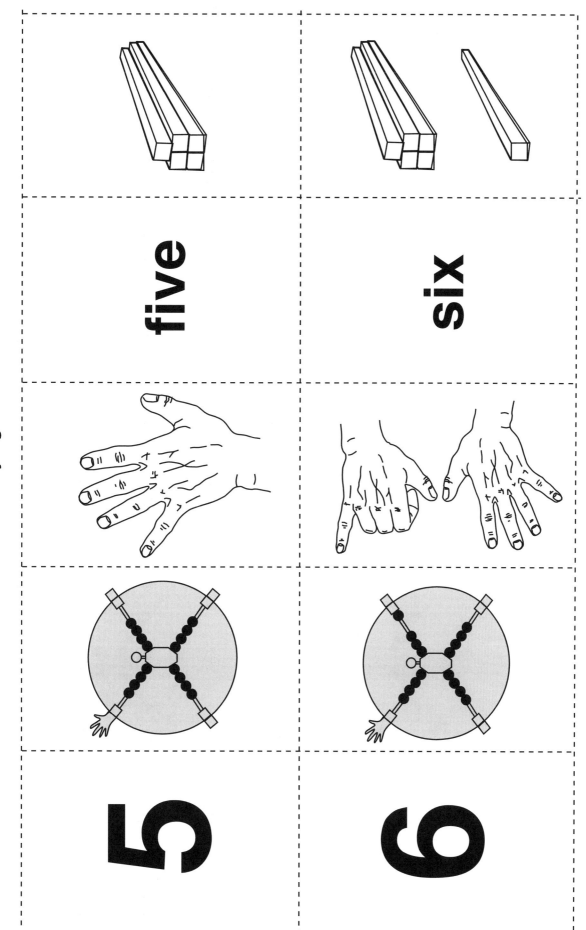

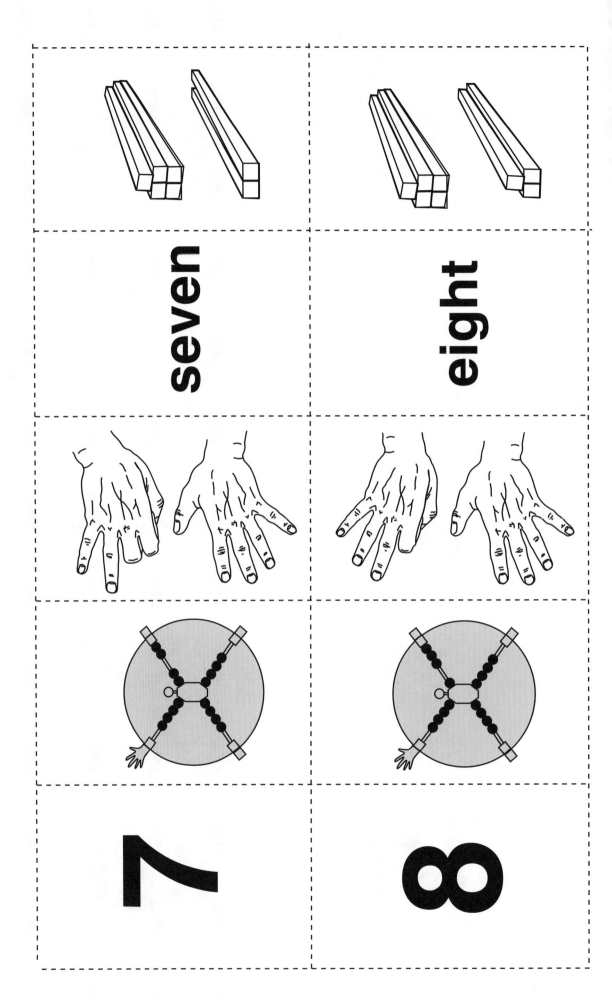

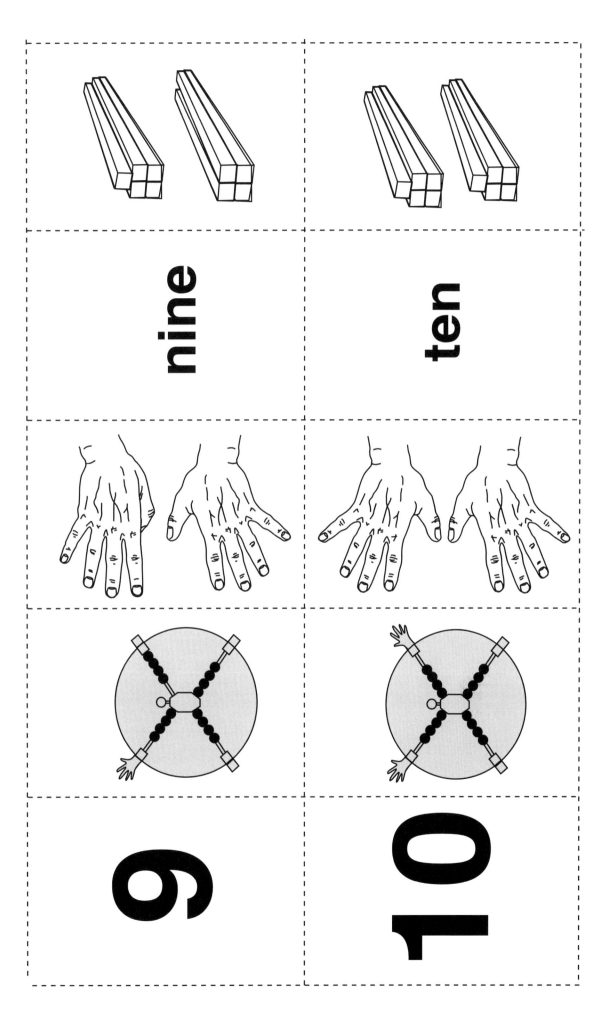

nine

ten

9

10

Activity 13:
Gone Fishing

This game continues to teach students about the ecology of Bristol Bay. In particular, they learn about the relationship of black-legged kittiwake chicks and the abundance of marine life. While learning this they have to solve multiple-step problems.

Goals

- To demonstrate food as one of the limiting factors to a seabird population

- Students role play as kittiwakes and "go fishing" (surface feeding) with chopsticks

- Solve two-step problems

Materials

- Sheet of blank paper (one per group of four students)
- Chopsticks (two per student)
- Washtub or other large container filled with water (one per group of four)
- Pieces of foam per tub (from packing boxes, unifix cubes, or one-centimeter interlocking cubes as substitutes) (twenty-one per group of four)

Duration

One class period.

Instructions

1. Discuss with students the idea that all living things need food, water, and shelter. Seabirds primarily eat small fish. When they have chicks, they must also find fish to feed their young.

2. Divide the class into groups of four. One student will be a recorder and the remaining three will be kittiwakes, equipped with chopsticks as beaks and a strong appetite for fish.

3. Place twenty-one pieces of foam in the tub. Each piece of foam represents one fish.

4. **Round one:** Two students play a nesting pair of kittiwakes. The third student is rolled up, pretending to be an egg in a nest. The "parents" must each collect five fish for themselves in order to survive. Have the two "parent" kittiwakes fish in the tub (ocean) with their chopsticks. After they catch them, return the ten fish to the tub to simulate fish reproduction. The fourth student records how many fish are left in the ocean (twenty-one fish). Have students from various groups share what and how they recorded how many fish the kittiwakes ate. Have students describe how they determined how many fish are left. If some students are having difficulty with this problem, have other students help them. **An adult kittiwake eats five fish.**

5. **Round two:** The egg has hatched, and the parents must now care for their new chick. Each adult must collect seven fish, of which they will eat five and feed two fish to their chick. The chick gets two fish from each parent, for a total of four fish. Have the parents fish with their chopsticks until they catch a total of fourteen. Have them place the chick's eggs in a "nest," i.e., a sheet of paper with a circle drawn on it. Return ten fish to the ocean to simulate fish reproduction. Have the fourth student record the number of fish in the ocean (seventeen). **Chick kittiwake eats four fish.**

6. **Round three:** The chick has fledged and is now old enough to feed itself (use its chopsticks). Each kittiwake, parents and fledged chick, must collect five fish. After this is accomplished, return ten fish to the ocean. Record the number of fish left in the ocean (twelve). Have students explain what is happening to the fish? Is there a pattern? **A fledged chick eats five fish.**

7. Continue. If there are not enough fish, the chick will die. Have the students discuss the life cycle of living things and think of ways that the fish and the birds could be in balance.

8. As activity leader, you can modify the game by changing the environmental conditions to make it as complicated as you wish. For example, explain that a storm has brought in nutrients and the fish now have a lot of plankton to eat; this has increased their numbers. Put ten more fish into the ocean.

9. After playing the game for a few rounds, have the recorders share their data and discuss the kittiwakes' experiences. Discuss how the kittiwakes' population size was limited by the quantity of fish available to them for feeding.

Activity 14:
Drumming, Hearing, and Placing
(Practice Activity)

The following activity will help reinforce the students' growing understanding of grouping and place values. Drumming introduces them to another learning modality by connecting sounds to grouping. In a game-like format, students will use three different "drum beats," with each drumbeat at a different dynamic level. (In music, dynamics refers to the variation of intensity in a sound.) A soft drumbeat will represent ones, a stronger one fives, and the strongest one twenties. The drummer can play a game, such as Guess My Number, in which each different combination of beats represents a different number. Have the students take turns beating out the numbers, and the other students will determine which number is being played.

Goals

- To reinforce the concepts of grouping by twenties and subgroups of five, both on paper and mentally

- To use a base twenty place-value chart

- To associate the numbers with combinations of drumbeats, based on ones, fives, and twenties

Materials

- Drums or drum substitutes (coffee cans) (one per group)
- Handout, Twenties, Fives, and Ones Place Value Chart (one per pair of students)
- Interlocking cubes or beads in three different colors (one-centimeter) (ten of each color per pair of students)
- Hat (one per group)
- Paper (several sheets per group)
- Scissors (one per group)

Instructions for Playing the Game

Demonstration

1. Demonstrate by beating the drum softly and having the students copy the beat by clapping. Tell the students that this "beat" will equal one. Repeat the drumbeat and say "one." Beat out a second, longer and stronger drumbeat, and have students copy it by clapping. Tell the students that this beat will equal five. Repeat the drumbeat and say "five." Introduce a third drumbeat that is even stronger and louder, and again have the students copy it. Tell the students that this beat will be equal to twenty. Repeat the drumbeat and say "twenty."

2. Practice by beating one of the three kinds of drumbeats. Have the students respond by clapping at a similar decibel level, then guess which number the beat represents.

3. Drum a brief succession of beats such as one loud beat, two medium beats, and one soft beat. Have the students repeat the pattern by clapping and then have them guess the number the pattern represents.

4. Have the students work in pairs and distribute the Twenties, Fives and Ones Place Value chart and three colors of interlocking cubes to each pair.

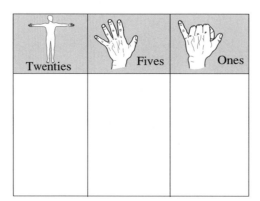

Fig. 14.1: Twenties, fives, and ones place-value chart

5. Designate one color cube to represent ones, a second color to represent fives, and a third to represent twenties.

6. Introduce the students to the game Guess My Number. Tell them that you will beat out a number on the drum and that they will need to listen very carefully, guess the number, then place the appropriately colored cubes in the appropriate column of the chart, either in the ones (soft beat), in the fives (medium strong beat) or in the twenties (strong beat) unit to indicate the number drummed out. Then, ask the students to say what number the drum beats represented. Practice this for a few minutes.

Fig. 14.2: Henry Alakayak and Anecia Lomack "drumming numbers"

Playing

6. Break into pairs or small groups.

8. Hand out a drum (coffee can) to each group. One student beats out a number. Ask the other students in the group to place their cubes onto the grouping chart, to show which number was drummed out.

9. Continue, so that each group member has at least three turns to drum.

Variation One

1. One student in the group makes one kind of beat; the second drummer makes a beat of his or her own choosing; the third does the same, and so on. The students then must decipher the number that they collectively made and represent it on their place value charts.

Cultural Note

Drumming is an important part of Yup'ik culture. Yup'ik drums are large, round, and flat, with a handle like a frying pan. They are held by the handle, and the drummer beats the drum with a straight wooden stick, often made of a peeled willow branch or a dowel. Traditionally, the drums were made of animal hide stretched over a wood hoop. Modern drums are often made of white nylon fabric stretched over a wooden hoop. In this activity, you will be using a traditional activity in a nontraditional way. The Yup'ik do not drum out numbers, but Yup'ik drumming will be used in this activity to do so.

Fig. 14.3: Yup'ik drum and stick

2. For example, student A drums a soft beat, student B drums another soft beat, and student C drums a loud beat. Collectively, they have made the number 22. Everyone should mark this number on his/her place value charts.

3. Continue this process for at least five rounds.

Variation Two

1. The drummer must tell each student his or her "number" after beating it out. The other group members verify for accuracy. After a drummer has made it through three numbers, students select a new drummer.

2. If the students require further practice, give each group several pieces of paper, some scissors, and a hat. Have the students cut out forty small squares of paper and write the numbers 1 through 40 on the squares. Each square gets only one number. Have them put the squares in a hat. Have them draw a number from a hat, and have the drummer beat it out. Have the group members represent it on their place value charts.

Teacher Note

Music, percussion in particular, depends on timing. Timing is developed through practice and counting. This activity provides students with an opportunity to practice working in base twenty through drumming.

Twenties, Fives, and Ones Place Value Chart

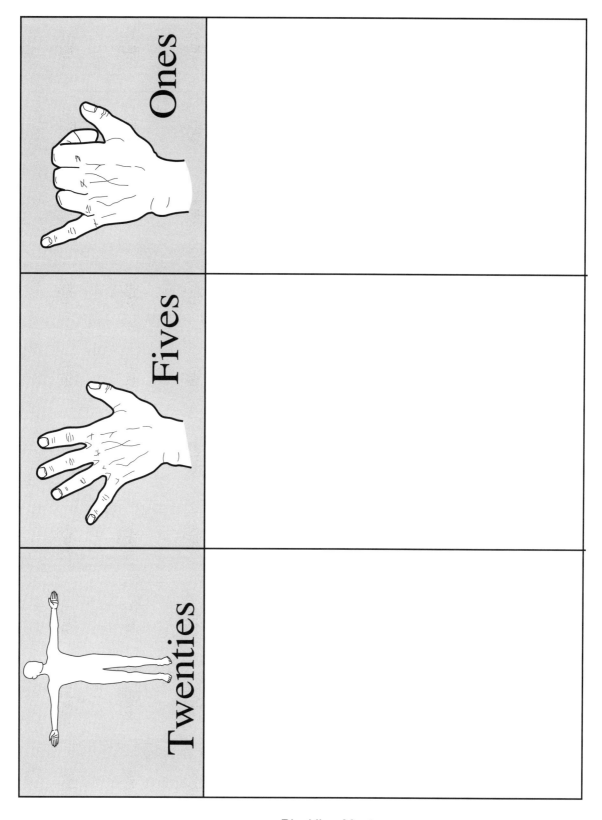

Section 4

Coming Home:

Travelling Back to the Village

Activity 15:
Storing, Sorting, and Counting the Eggs

Read chapter 9, "Counting and Sorting the Eggs." Today's activity involves sorting eggs following the way Yup'ik people may sort them.

Goals

- To count the number of eggs

- To use an abacus to show quantities as two-digit numbers

- To sort and classify eggs according to specific criteria

Materials

- Story book, *Egg Island*
- Poster, Egg Island Map with grid
- Transparency, Sorting Eggs
- Paperclips (two different sizes, twenty per each size) for the teacher demonstration
- Masking tape
- Handout, Sorting Chart (one per group)
- Shoebox or other "bucket" (one per pair of students)
- "Eggs" (may substitute with washers, pennies, etc.) (thirteen walnuts and forty-five almonds per pair of students)
- Egg cartons or paper cups (four per pair of students)
- Handout, Twenties, Fives, and Ones Place Value Chart (one per pair of students)
- Interlocking cubes (three different colors, ten of each color, per pair of students)
- Yup'ik abacus from Activity 10 that students made (one per student)
- Felt pen (one per group)

Duration

One class period.

Vocabulary

Two-digit or double-digit number—a number from 10 to 99

Cultural Note

Old eggs *(yuk)* means a person. The egg is developing into a bird. These are called the old ones. They also float because they are lighter than the other eggs. When egg gathering, people try not to choose the old eggs. Not all of the old eggs will cook.

Instructions

1. Read *Egg Island,* chapter 9, and discuss the return trip.

2. Show the students the Egg Island poster, and let the students locate where today's story is taking place.

Counting and Sorting the Eggs

3. Use the transparency Sorting Eggs to show one way of sorting. Next, demonstrate sorting by using two different-sized paper clips. Use approximately twenty paper clips of each type and have two of each type be "old," representing old eggs. To create "old eggs" put masking tape on the paper clip. Demonstrate grouping the clips into four different categories.

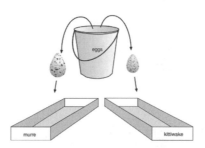

Fig. 15.1: Sorting eggs

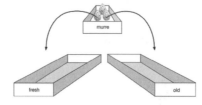
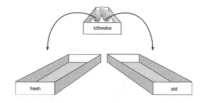

Fig. 15.2: Sorting eggs into murre and kittiwake, then old and new

4. Have the big clips represent the murre eggs, the little clips represent the kittiwake eggs, and those with tape represent the old eggs. Count the number of clips in each group and mark this number in the appropriate box in the transparency Sorting Chart.

Murre		Kittiwake	
fresh number	old number	fresh number	old number

Fig. 15.3: Sorting chart

5. Have students work in groups of two. Hand out to each group one bucket (shoe box), filled with the thirteen walnuts and forty-five almonds. Hand out a felt pen to each group and have the students mark one walnut and five almonds with the pen to represent old eggs. Hand out four egg cartons (or paper cups if you don't have enough cartons to go around) and one sorting chart per group. Have the walnuts be murre eggs and the almonds be kittiwake eggs.

6. Today's challenge is for each group of students to sort and count the eggs. Have the students sort and count the number of murre and kittiwake eggs. Then have the students further sort the eggs by fresh and old (those that are marked are old). The students may use the egg cartons to help them sort. Each group should end up with four categories: murre old and new and kittiwake old and new.

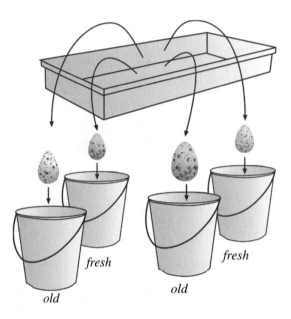

Fig. 15.4: Sorting fresh and old

7. Hand out the Twenties, Fives, and Ones Place Value chart, interlocking cubes, and abacus to each group. Students should use the chart with the cubes, or the abacus, to count the number of eggs.

8. Have each group describe its procedures for sorting, grouping, and tallying (adding) the eggs. Have each group show the totals arrived at and how they grouped and displayed those numbers on the abacus and/or the place value chart.

Sorting Eggs

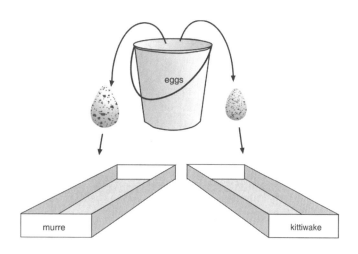

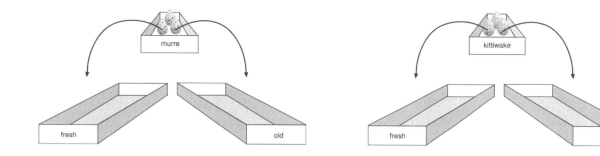

Twenties, Fives, and Ones Place Value Chart

Twenties	Fives	Ones

Sorting Chart

Murre		Kittiwake	
fresh number	old number	fresh number	old number

Activity 16:
Distributing Eggs to the Elders: Estimating, Grouping, Adding, and Subtracting

Today is the last day that Jennie will be in the village. Before she leaves and returns home, the family will give eggs to elders who can no longer travel to Egg Island. Distributing eggs to elders will involve the students in subtracting and in keeping track of the total number of eggs.

Goals

- Use of an abacus

- Work in base twenty

- Invent algorithms for adding and subtracting

Materials

- Story book, *Egg Island*
- Poster, Egg Island Map with grid
- Handout, Egg Island Map (from Activity 1)
- Shoebox or other "bucket" (one per pair of students)
- "Eggs" (may substitute with washers, pennies, etc.) (thirteen walnuts and forty-five almonds per pair of students)
- Yup'ik abacus from Activity 10 that students made (one per student)
- Handout, Twenties, Fives and Ones Place Value-Chart (one per pair of students)
- Interlocking cubes (three different colors, ten of each color, per pair of students)
- Handout, Distributing Eggs (one per pair of students)

Duration

One class period.

Instructions

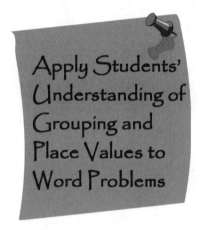

Apply Students' Understanding of Grouping and Place Values to Word Problems

1. Read chapter 10, "Heading Back and Distributing the Eggs."

2. Have the students work in pairs. Have the students locate where Jennie is today on the Egg Island map.

3. Hand out a bucket (shoe box) filled with "eggs" (thirteen walnuts and forty-five almonds or any other objects that can serve as eggs) to each pair. Hand out the abacus, the Twenties, Fives, and Ones Place Value chart, and the set of interlocking cubes to each pair.

4. Hand out the Distributing Eggs worksheet. As the students answer the questions, they may want to use their abaci and their Twenties, Fives, and Ones charts. Remember: walnuts represent murre eggs and almonds represent kittiwake eggs.

5. Demonstrate how to answer the first question on the worksheet. Show one way of solving the problem, such as removing six eggs from the total of twenty-five eggs to discover the remaining number of eggs. Ask students to suggest other ways to answer the question. For example, students may group twenty-five eggs into five groups of five and subtract six eggs by making one group of five plus one. Further, students may represent twenty-five on their abacus and then subtract six from it.

6. Have students work in pairs. Encourage them to invent their own strategies for solving the problems. Observe what kind of strategies they used. Question the pairs so that they explain their strategies.

7. Have some pairs share their way of solving their problems. Encourage multiple solution strategies—paper and pencil, abacus, etc.

Distributing Eggs

1. Suppose you have twenty-five eggs. Your aunt is no longer able to visit Egg Island and has run out of eggs. You give her six eggs. How many eggs do you have left?

2. Suppose you started with thirteen murre and forty-five kittiwake eggs. How many murre and kittiwake eggs are left if we give two elders each six murre and six kittiwake eggs?

3. Suppose you started with thirteen murre and forty-five kittiwake eggs. How many total eggs are left if we give two elders each four murre and twelve kittiwake eggs?

4.   You collected thirteen murre and forty-five kittiwake eggs. You now have six murre and twenty-four kittiwake eggs. How many murre and how many kittiwake eggs did you give away?

5.   You gave twelve eggs to an elder. You now have twenty-four eggs left. How many eggs did you start with?

6.   After an hour of egg gathering, you have gathered five murre and ten kittiwake eggs. How many more do you need to gather to have a total of thirty murre and fifty kittiwake eggs?

Twenties, Fives, and Ones Place-Value Chart

Twenties	Fives	Ones

Activity 17:
Representing Numbers to One Hundred on a Yup'ik Abacus

In today's lesson, students will continue to use the abacus for numbers up to one hundred.

Students' competency and facility in using the abacus can be strengthened beyond this module by allowing them to use it as they solve addition and subtraction problems. The more practical use students can make of the abacus, the more likely they will learn how to use it and understand place values and the concept of "exchange."

Goal

- Practice using the Yup'ik abacus

Materials

- Poster, Egg Island Map with grid
- Yup'ik abacus from Activity 10 that students made (one per student) or special Yup'ik Abacus that counts to one hundred (one per group)
- Handout, Abacus Worksheet (one per student)

Instructions

1. Have students work in pairs and give each pair the Yup'ik abacus that counts up to one hundred. If your class does not have this abacus (which is shown on the following page) then have students work in groups of five so they can use their one to twenty abacus (which they made in Activity 10). In this way, each group can represent numbers to a hundred.

2. Students will learn about the Yup'ik values of reciprocity and helping the elders. Have a brief discussion about today's story. Use the map of Egg Island and have the students locate the village.

3. Hand out the Abacus sorksheet. The special Yup'ik abacus that counts up to one hundred in the worksheet looks different than the one the students have previously used. Each bowling pin shape represents the number 20. When twenty is reached, the pin is pushed from the left to the right.

4. Have the students use their abaci to represent the numbers indicated on the worksheet, and have them also write out how they represented each number. For example, 28 can be represented in multiple ways. Below is one way:

   20 + 5 + 3 = 28

5. Let the students practice for ten to fifteen minutes, then go over their work and have different pairs of students explain their procedures for grouping. Again, it is important to have students clarify their thinking. Other students may question them and can also probe their thinking.

6. To conclude the lesson, have each group make up a problem and have the other groups solve it. Discuss strategies and answers. Below is a sample of a student's work.

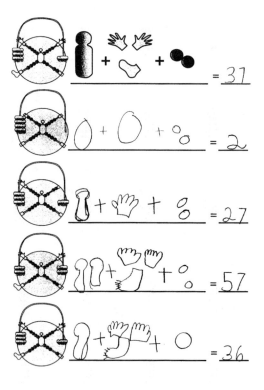

Fig. 17.1: Example of student's work with the abacus to 100

Abacus Worksheet

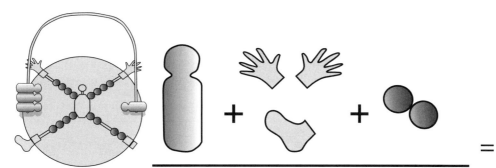

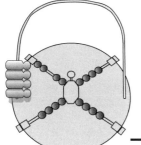

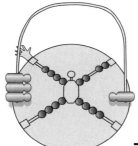

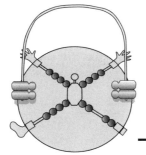

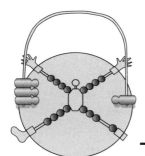

Activity 18:
Storing the Eggs;
Grouping by Twelves

Students will store the eggs in standard (one dozen) egg cartons. In today's activity students continue to understand grouping and place value. They work with groups of twelve and groups of ten objects and then use a place-value-like system for noting their value.

Goals

- To represent numbers in a twelves and tens system

- To group by twelves

- To solve word problems by regrouping and equal exchange

Materials

- Story book, *Egg Island*
- Egg cartons or handout, Template of an Egg Carton (two per student)
- Transparency, Template of an Egg Carton
- Paperclips (Eggs) (thirty per pair of students)
- Transparency, Twelves and Ones Chart
- Transparency, Tens and Ones Chart
- Box
- Handout, Grouping by Twelves and Tens (per pair of students)

Duration

One class period.

Vocabulary

Dozen—grouping by twelves

Preparation

Bring in enough egg cartons for the class.

Instructions

1. Read the final chapter of *Egg Island,* "Back to the City." Hold a discussion with the students about Jennie's experiences and what she may have learned.

2. Hand out four egg cartons to each group of two students. If there aren't enough egg cartons, make four copies of the egg carton template to distribute to each group. Students will be storing eggs in egg cartons because this has become a customary way to store eggs. The teacher should hold up an egg carton or the template and ask, "How many eggs does this hold?"

Fig. 18.1: Egg Carton

3. Demonstrate how to sort fourteen eggs into groups of twelve. Using the transparency of the egg template, place twelve "eggs" (clips) into the twelve circles. Then show the students that twelve eggs fit the carton and that two eggs are left over.

Twelves	Ones	
		Total Number
√	√ √	14

Fig. 18.2: Twelves and ones chart

4. Using the transparency of the Twelves and Ones chart, represent the number 14 by marking the appropriate columns. Have students discuss the relationship between twelve individual eggs placed in the egg carton and one tally mark in the twelves column.

5. Now demonstrate how to sort the fourteen eggs into groups of ten. Using the transparency of the Tens and Ones chart, represent the number fourteen by marking the appropriate columns.

Tens	Ones
√	√ √ √ √

Fig. 18.3: Tens and ones chart

6. Hand out a box with thirty paper clips to each group.

7. Have the students put all their "eggs" into the egg cartons. How many eggs are left outside of the carton?

8. Ask the class to express the number of eggs as groups of twelve. They should say, "We have used two egg cartons, and have six eggs left over." Tell them that grouping by twelves is the way eggs are grouped and stored.

9. Ask the class to express the number of eggs as groups of ten. They should say, "There are three groups of ten."

10. Hand out the Grouping by Twelves and Tens worksheet to each student pair and have the students fill it out.

11. Observe how students solve these problems. Probe their thinking.

12. When students have completed the problems, have them share their strategies.

Teacher Note

When students are asked what the "3" in 36 means, many students represent it with three unit blocks. When asked what the "6" in 36 means many students represent it with unit blocks. Facilitate students' understanding of place value by asking such questions as: "If you add these blocks together, how many do you have?" The student might say "9."

Then you could ask the student, "but I thought the number was equal to 36? Something seems wrong; could you explain this?"

Grouping by Twelves and Tens

1. How many egg cartons are needed to store thirty eggs? How many eggs are left over? Show your answer on the Twelves and Ones chart.

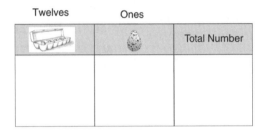

Twelves	Ones	Total Number

2. You gave away twelve eggs. You started with thirty. How many are left? Show your answer on the twelves and ones chart.

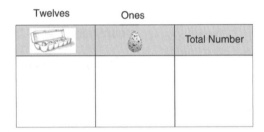

Twelves	Ones	Total Number

3. Mary gave away twelve eggs to an elder. Now, she has twenty-four eggs. How many did she have to begin with? Show your answer on the twelves and ones chart.

Twelves	Ones	Total Number

Grouping by Twelves and Tens (continued)

4. Suppose you gave away six eggs each to two elders. You started with thirty-eight eggs. How many do you have? Show your answer on the Twelves and Ones Chart.

Twelves	Ones	Total Number

5. Suppose you ran out of egg cartons for storing eggs, but you find a box that has ten compartments for storing the eggs. You have to store thirty-two eggs. Draw a picture that shows the eggs being stored in groups of ten.

6. Represent the value thirty-six on the tens and ones chart below.

Tens	Ones

Template of an Egg Carton

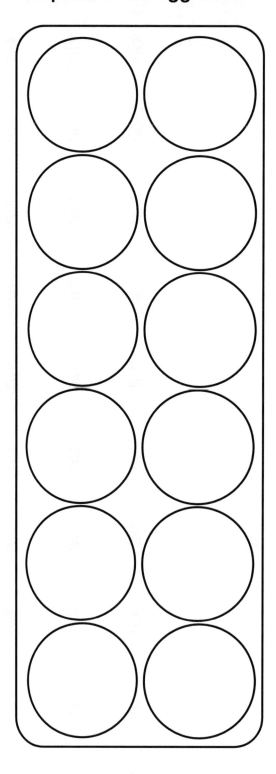

Twelves and Ones Chart

Twelves	Ones	
		Total Number

Tens and Ones Chart

Tens	Ones	Total number

Activity 19:
Sharing: An Important Part of Subsistence Gathering

This final lesson affords an excellent time for the students' parents to be invited into class. Use this opportunity to have students share some of what they've learned.

Invite the Parents

1. Invite the parents to share in what the students have learned about Egg Island and the math of grouping by twenties, twelves, and fives.

2. Have food, particularly egg dishes, to share.

3. Have students demonstrate what they have learned about grouping by using their bodies, the abaci, and other methods. Have them use the base-twenty abacus and group in twelves. Have the students teach their parents how to use the Yup'ik abacus.